Jacob Abbott

History of Alfred the Great

The Founder of the British Monarchy

Jacob Abbott

History of Alfred the Great
The Founder of the British Monarchy

ISBN/EAN: 9783743419124

Manufactured in Europe, USA, Canada, Australia, Japa

Cover: Foto ©ninafisch / pixelio.de

Manufactured and distributed by brebook publishing software (www.brebook.com)

Jacob Abbott

History of Alfred the Great

Makers of History

Alfred the Great

BY

JACOB ABBOTT

WITH ENGRAVINGS

NEW YORK AND LONDON
HARPER & BROTHERS PUBLISHERS
1904

Entered, according to Act of Congress, in the year one thousand eight hundred and forty-nine, by

HARPER & BROTHERS,

In the Clerk's Office of the District Court of the Southern District of New York.

Copyright, 1877, by JACOB ABBOTT.

PREFACE.

It is the object of this series of histories to present a clear, distinct, and connected narrative of the lives of those great personages who have in various ages of the world made themselves celebrated as leaders among mankind, and, by the part they have taken in the public affairs of great nations, have exerted the widest influence on the history of the human race. The end which the author has had in view is twofold: first, to communicate such information in respect to the subjects of his narratives as is important for the general reader to posesss; and, secondly, to draw such moral lessons from the events described and the characters delineated as they may legitimately teach to the people of the present age. Though written in a direct and simple style, they are intended for, and addressed to, minds possessed of some considerable degree of maturity, for such minds only can fully appreciate the character and action which exhibits itself, as nearly all that is described in these volumes does, in close combination with the conduct and policy of governments, and the great events of international history.

CONTENTS.

Chapter	Page
I. THE BRITONS	13
II. THE ANGLO-SAXONS	34
III. THE DANES	57
IV. ALFRED'S EARLY YEARS	76
V. THE STATE OF ENGLAND	94
VI. ALFRED'S ACCESSION TO THE THRONE	115
VII. REVERSES	131
VIII. THE SECLUSION	154
IX. REASSEMBLING OF THE ARMY	172
X. THE VICTORY OVER THE DANES	190
XI. THE REIGN	209
XII. THE CLOSE OF LIFE	227

ENGRAVINGS.

	Page
WALL OF SEVERUS	31
SAXON MILITARY CHIEF	41
THE SEA KINGS	65
LOTHBROC AND HIS FALCON	103
ANCIENT CORONATION CHAIR	133
THE FIRST BRITISH FLEET	148
ALFRED WATCHING THE CAKES	161
PORTRAIT OF ALFRED	208
HASTINGS BESIEGED IN THE CHURCH	229

ALFRED THE GREAT.

CHAPTER I.

THE BRITONS.

Alfred the founder of the British monarchy.

ALFRED THE GREAT figures in history as the founder, in some sense, of the British monarchy. Of that long succession of sovereigns who have held the scepter of that monarchy, and whose government has exerted so vast an influence on the condition and welfare of mankind, he was not, indeed, actually the first. There were several lines of insignificant princes before him, who governed such portions of the kingdom as they individually possessed, more like semi-savage chieftains than English kings. Alfred followed these by the principle of hereditary right, and spent his life in laying broad and deep the foundations on which the enormous superstructure of the British empire has since been reared. If the tales respecting his character and deeds which have come down

Hereditary succession. *The fabulous age of history*

to us are at all worthy of belief, he was an honest, conscientious, disinterested, and far-seeing statesman. If the system of hereditary succession would always furnish such sovereigns for mankind, the principle of loyalty would have held its place much longer in the world than it is now likely to do, and great nations, now republican, would have been saved a vast deal of trouble and toil expended in the election of their rulers.

Although the period of King Alfred's reign seems a very remote one as we look back toward it from the present day, it was still eight hundred years after the Christian era that he ascended his throne. Tolerable authentic history of the British realm mounts up through these eight hundred years to the time of Julius Cæsar. Beyond this the ground is covered by a series of romantic and fabulous tales, pretending to be history, which extend back eight hundred years further to the days of Solomon; so that a much longer portion of the story of that extraordinary island comes before than since the days of Alfred. In respect, however to all that pertains to the interest and importance of the narrative, the exploits and the arrangements of Alfred are the beginning.

B.C. 800.] THE BRITONS. 15

Tradition.   The Trojan war.   Adventures of Æneas

The histories, in fact, of all nations, ancient and modern, run back always into misty regions of romance and fable. Before arts and letters arrived at such a state of progress as that public events could be recorded in writing, tradition was the only means of handing down the memory of events from generation to generation; and tradition, among semi-savages, changes every thing it touches into romantic and marvelous fiction.

The stories connected with the earliest discovery and settlement of Great Britain afford very good illustrations of the nature of these fabulous tales. The following may serve as a specimen:

At the close of the Trojan war,* Æneas retired with a company of Trojans, who escaped from the city with him, and, after a great variety of adventures, which Virgil has related, he landed and settled in Italy. Here, in process of time, he had a grandson named Silvius, who had a son named Brutus, Brutus being thus Æneas's great-grandson.

One day, while Brutus was hunting in the forests, he accidentally killed his father with

---

* For some account of the circumstances connected with this war, see our history of Alexander, chapter vi.

an arrow. His father was at that time King
of Alba—a region of Italy near the spot on
which Rome was subsequently built—and the
accident brought Brutus under such suspicions,
and exposed him to such dangers, that he fled
from the country. After various wanderings
he at last reached Greece, where he collected a
number of Trojan followers, whom he found
roaming about the country, and formed them
into an army. With this half-savage force he
attacked a king of the country named Pandrasus. Brutus was successful in the war, and
Pandrasus was taken prisoner. This compelled Pandrasus to sue for peace, and peace was
concluded on the following very extraordinary
terms:

Pandrasus was to give Brutus his daughter
Imogena for a wife, and a fleet of ships as her
dowry. Brutus, on the other hand, was to take
his wife and all his followers on board of his
fleet, and sail away and seek a home in some
other quarter of the globe. This plan of a monarch's purchasing his own ransom and peace for
his realm from a band of roaming robbers, by
offering the leader of them his daughter for a
wife, however strange to our ideas, was very
characteristic of the times. Imogena must

have found it a hard alternative to choose between such a husband and such a father.

Brutus, with his fleet and his bride, betook themselves to sea, and within a short time landed on a deserted island, where they found the ruins of a city. Here there was an ancient temple of Diana, and an image of the goddess, which image was endued with the power of uttering oracular responses to those who consulted it with proper ceremonies and forms. Brutus consulted this oracle on the question in what land he should find a place of final settlement. His address to it was in ancient verse, which some chronicler has turned into English rhyme as follows:

"Goddess of shades and huntress, who at will
 Walk'st on the rolling sphere, and through the deep
On thy *third* reign, the earth look now and tell
 What land, what seat of rest thou bidd'st me seek?"

To which the oracle returned the following answer:

"Far to the west, in the ocean wide,
 Beyond the realm of Gaul a land there lies—
Sea-girt it lies—where giants dwelt of old.
 Now void, it fits thy people; thither bend
Thy course; there shalt thou find a lasting home."

It is scarcely necessary to say that this meant Britain. Brutus, following the directions which the oracle had given him, set sail from the island, and proceeded to the westward through the Mediterranean Sea. He arrived at the Pillars of Hercules. This was the name by which the Rock of Gibraltar and the corresponding promontory on the opposite coast, across the straits, were called in those days; these cliffs having been built, according to ancient tales, by Hercules, as monuments set up to mark the extreme limits of his western wanderings. Brutus passed through the strait, and then, turning northward, coasted along the shores of Spain.

At length, after enduring great privations and suffering, and encountering the extreme dangers to which their frail barks were necessarily exposed from the surges which roll in perpetually from the broad Atlantic Ocean upon the coast of Spain and into the Bay of Biscay they arrived safely on the shores of Britain. They landed and explored the interior. They found the island robed in the richest drapery of fruitfulness and verdure, but it was unoccupied by any thing human. There were wild beasts roaming in the forests, and the remains of a race of giants in dens and caves—monsters as diverse from humanity as the wolves. Brutus and his followers attacked all these occupants of the land. They drove the wild beasts into the mountains of Scotland and Wales, and killed the giants. The chief of them, whose name was Gogmagog, was hurled by one of Brutus's followers from the summit of one of the chalky cliffs which bound the island into the sea.

The island of Great Britain is in the latitude of Labrador, which on our side of the continent is the synonym for almost perpetual ice and snow; still these wandering Trojans found it a region of inexhaustible verdure, fruitfulness, and beauty; and as to its extent, though often, in modern times, called a little island, they found its green fields and luxuriant forests extending very far and wide over the sea. A length of nearly six hundred miles would seem almost to merit the name of continent, and the dimensions of this detached outpost of the habitable surface of the earth would never have been deemed inconsiderable, had it not been that the people, by the greatness of their exploits, of which the whole world has been the theater, have made the physical dimensions of their territory appear so small and insignificant in comparison. To Brutus and his companions the land appeared a world. It was nearly four hundred miles in breadth at the place where

Fertility and beauty of the island.   **Successors of Brutus.**

they landed, and, wandering northward, they found it extending, in almost undiminished beauty and fruitfulness, further than they had the disposition to explore it. They might have gone northward until the twilight scarcely disappeared in the summer nights, and have found the same verdure and beauty continuing to the end. There were broad and undulating plains in the southern regions of the island, and in the northern, green mountains and romantic glens; but all, plains, valleys, and mountains, were fertile and beautiful, and teeming with abundant sustenance for flocks, for herds, and for man.

Brutus accordingly established himself upon the island with all his followers, and founded a kingdom there, over which he reigned as the founder of a dynasty. Endless tales are told of the lives, and exploits, and quarrels of his successors down to the time of Cæsar. Conflicting claimants arose continually to dispute with each other for the possession of power; wars were made by one tribe upon another; cities, as they were called—though probably, in fact, they were only rude collections of hovels—were built, fortresses were founded, and rivers were named from princes or princesses drowned in them, in accidental journeys, or by the violence of rival claimants to their thrones. The pretended records contain a vast number of legends, of very little interest or value, as the reader will readily admit when we tell him that the famous story of King Lear is the most entertaining one in the whole collection. It is this:

There was a king in the line named Lear. He founded the city now called Leicester. He had three daughters, whose names were Gonilla, Regana, and Cordiella. Cordiella was her father's favorite child. He was, however, jealous of the affections of them all, and one day he called them to him, and asked them for some assurance of their love. The two eldest responded by making the most extravagant protestations. They loved their father a thousand times better than their own souls. They could not express, they said, the ardor and strength of their attachment, and called Heaven and earth to witness that these protestations were sincere.

Cordiella, all this time, stood meekly and silently by, and when her father asked her how it was with her, she replied, "Father, my love toward you is as my duty bids. What can a father ask, or a daughter promise more? They who pretend beyond this only flatter."

The king, who was old and childish, was much pleased with the manifestation of love offered by Gonilla and Regana, and thought that the honest Cordiella was heartless and cold He treated her with greater and greater neglect and finally decided to leave her without any portion whatever, while he divided his kingdom between the other two, having previously married them to princes of high rank. Cordiella was, however, at last made choice of for a wife by a French prince, who, it seems, knew better than the old king how much more to be relied upon was unpretending and honest truth than empty and extravagant profession He married the portionless Cordiella, and took her with him to the Continent.

The old king now having given up his kingdom to his eldest daughters, they managed, by artifice and maneuvering, to get every thing else away from him, so that he became wholly dependent upon them, and had to live with them by turns. This was not all; for, at the instigation of their husbands, they put so many indignities and affronts upon him, that his life at length became an intolerable burden, and finally he was compelled to leave the realm altogether, and in his destitution and distress he

| Julius Cæsar. | His conquest of Great Britain. |

went for refuge and protection to his rejected daughter Cordiella. She received her father with the greatest alacrity and affection. She raised an army to restore him to his rights, and went in person with him to England to assist him in recovering them. She was successful. The old king took possession of his throne again, and reigned in peace for the remainder of his days. The story is of itself nothing very remarkable, though Shakspeare has immortalized it by making it the subject of one of his tragedies.

Centuries passed away, and at length the great Julius Cæsar, who was extending the Roman power in every direction, made his way across the Channel, and landed in England. The particulars of this invasion are described in our history of Julius Cæsar. The Romans retained possession of the island, in a greater or less degree, for four hundred years.

They did not, however, hold it in peace all this time. They became continually involved in difficulties and contests with the native Britons, who could ill brook the oppressions of such merciless masters as Roman generals always proved in the provinces which they pretended to govern. One of the most formidable rebellions that the Romans had to encounter during their disturbed and troubled sway in Britain was led on by a woman. Her name was Boadicea. Boadicea, like almost all other heroines, was coarse and repulsive in appearance. She was tall and masculine in form. The tones of her voice were harsh, and she had the countenance of a savage. Her hair was yellow. It might have been beautiful if it had been neatly arranged, and had shaded a face which possessed the gentle expression that belongs properly to woman. It would then have been called golden. As it was, hanging loosely below her waist and streaming in the wind, it made the wearer only look the more frightful. Still, Boadicea was not by any means indifferent to the appearance she made in the eyes of beholders. She evinced her desire to make a favorable impression upon others, in her own peculiar way, it is true, but in one which must have been effective, considering what sort of beholders they were in whose eyes she figured. She was dressed in a gaudy coat, wrought of various colors, with a sort of mantle buttoned over it. She wore a great gold chain about her neck, and held an ornamented spear in her hand. Thus equipped, she appeared at the head of an army

Death of Boadicea. **Final subjugation of the Britons.**

of a hundred thousand men, and gathering them around her, she ascended a mound of earth and harangued them—that is, as many as could stand within reach of her voice—arousing them to sentiments of revenge against their hated oppressors, and urging them to the highest pitch of determination and courage for the approaching struggle. Boadicea had reason to deem the Romans her implacable foes. They had robbed her of her treasures, deprived her of her kingdom, imprisoned her, scourged her, and inflicted the worst possible injuries upon her daughters. These things had driven the wretched mother to a perfect phrensy of hate, and aroused her to this desperate struggle for redress and revenge. But all was in vain. In encountering the spears of Roman soldiery, she was encountering the very hardest and sharpest steel that a cruel world could furnish. Her army was conquered, and she killed herself by taking poison in her despair.

By struggles such as these the contest between the Romans and the Britons was carried on for many generations; the Romans conquering at every trial, until, at length, the Britons learned to submit without further resistance to their sway. In fact, there gradually came upon the stage, during the progress of these centuries, a new power, acting as an enemy to both the Picts and Scots; hordes of lawless barbarians, who inhabited the mountains and morasses of Scotland and Ireland. These terrible savages made continual irruptions into the southern country for plunder, burning and destroying, as they retired, whatever they could not carry away. They lived in impregnable and almost inaccessible fastnesses, among dark glens and precipitous mountains, and upon gloomy islands surrounded by iron-bound coasts and stormy seas. The Roman legions made repeated attempts to hunt them out of these retreats, but with very little success. At length a line of fortified posts was established across the island, near where the boundary line now lies between England and Scotland; and by guarding this line, the Roman generals who had charge of Britain attempted to protect the inhabitants of the southern country, who had learned at length to submit peaceably to their sway.

One of the most memorable events which occurred during the time that the Romans held possession of the island of Britain was the visit of one of the emperors to this northern extrem-

Visit of the Emperor Severus. His dissolute sons.

ity of his dominions. The name of this emperor was Severus. He was powerful and prosperous at home, but his life was embittered by one great calamity, the dissolute character and the perpetual quarrels of his sons. To remove them from Rome, where they disgraced both themselves and their father by their vicious lives, and the ferocious rivalry and hatred they bore to each other, Severus planned an excursion to Britain, taking them with him, in the hope of turning their minds into new channels of thought, and awakening in them some new and nobler ambition.

At the time when Severus undertook this expedition, he was advanced in age and very infirm. He suffered much from the gout, so that he was unable to travel by any ordinary conveyance, and was borne, accordingly, almost all the way upon a litter. He crossed the Channel with his army, and, leaving one of his sons in command in the south part of the island, he advanced with the other, at the head of an enormous force, determined to push boldly forward into the heart of Scotland, and to bring the war with the Picts and Scots to an effectual end.

He met, however, with very partial success. His soldiers became entangled in bogs and morasses; they fell into ambuscades; they suffered every degree of privation and hardship for want of water and of food, and were continually entrapped by their enemies in situations where they had to fight in small numbers and at a great disadvantage. Then, too, the aged and feeble general was kept in a continual fever of anxiety and trouble by Bassianus, the son whom he had brought with him to the north. The dissoluteness and violence of his character were not changed by the change of scene. He formed plots and conspiracies against his father's authority; he raised mutinies in the army; he headed riots; and he was finally detected in a plan for actually assassinating his father. Severus, when he discovered this last enormity of wickedness, sent for his son to come to his imperial tent. He laid a naked sword before him, and then, after bitterly reproaching him with his undutiful and ungrateful conduct, he said, "If you wish to kill me, do it now. Here I stand, old, infirm, and helpless. You are young and strong, and can do it easily. I am ready Strike the blow."

Of course Bassianus shrunk from his father's reproaches, and went away without committing the crime to which he was thus reproachfully invited; but his character remained unchanged; and this constant trouble, added to all the other difficulties which Severus encountered, prevented his accomplishing his object of thoroughly conquering his northern foes. He made a sort of peace with them, and retiring south to the line of fortified posts which had been previously established, he determined to make it a fixed and certain boundary by building upon it a permanent wall. He put the whole force of his army upon the work, and in one or two years, as is said, he completed the structure. It is known in history as the Wall of Severus; and so solid, substantial, and permanent was the work, that the traces of it have not entirely disappeared to the present day.

The wall extended across the island, from the mouth of the Tyne, on the German Ocean, to the Solway Frith—nearly seventy miles. It was twelve feet high, and eight feet wide. It was faced with substantial masonry on both sides, the intermediate space being likewise filled in with stone. When it crossed bays or morasses, piles were driven to serve as a foundation. Of course, such a wall as this, by itself, would be no defense. It was to be garrisoned by soldiers, being intended, in fact, only as a

| Stations. | Castles. | Turrets. | Ditch. | Military road |

means to enable a smaller number of troops than would otherwise be necessary to guard the line. For these soldiers there were built great fortresses at intervals along the wall, wherever a situation was found favorable for such structures. These were called *stations*. The stations were occupied by garrisons of troops, and small towns of artificers and laborers soon sprung up around them. Between the stations, at smaller intervals, were other smaller fortresses called castles, intended as places of defense, and rallying points in case of an attack, but not for garrisons of any considerable number of men. Then, between the castles, at smaller intervals still, were turrets, used as watch-towers and posts for sentinels. Thus the whole line of the wall was every where defended by armed men. The whole number thus employed in the defense of this extraordinary rampart was said to be ten thousand. There was a broad, deep, and continuous ditch on the northern side of the wall, to make the impediment still greater for the enemy, and a spacious and well-constructed military road on the southern side, on which troops, stores, wagons, and baggage of every kind could be readily transported along the line, from one end to the other.

WALL OF SEVERUS.

Decline of the Roman empire. *Distress of the Britons.*

The wall was a good defense as long as Roman soldiers remained to guard it. But in process of time—about two centuries after Severus's day—the Roman empire itself began to decline, even in the very seat and center of its power; and then, to preserve their own capital from destruction, the government were obliged to call their distant armies home. The wall was left to the Britons; but they could not defend it. The Picts and Scots, finding out the change, renewed their assaults. They battered down the castles; they made breaches here and there in the wall; they built vessels, and, passing round by sea across the mouth of the Solway Frith and of the River Tyne, they renewed their old incursions for plunder and destruction. The Britons, in extreme distress, sent again and again to recall the Romans to their aid, and they did, in fact, receive from them some occasional and temporary succor. At length, however, all hope of help from this quarter failed, and the Britons, finding their condition desperate, were compelled to resort to a desperate remedy, the nature of which will be explained in the next chapter.

Constitutional and connate differences among men.

Chapter II.

The Anglo-Saxons

ANY one who will look around upon the families of his acquaintance will observe that family characteristics and resemblances prevail not only in respect to stature, form, expression of countenance, and other outward and bodily tokens, but also in regard to the constitutional temperaments and capacities of the soul. Sometimes we find a group in which high intellectual powers and great energy of action prevail for many successive generations, and in all the branches into which the original stock divides; in other cases, the hereditary tendency is to gentleness and harmlessness of character, with a full development of all the feelings and sensibilities of the soul. Others, again, exhibit congenital tendencies to great physical strength and hardihood, and to powers of muscular exertion and endurance. These differences, notwithstanding all the exceptions and irregularities connected with them, are obviously, where they exist, deeply seated and

Characteristics of nations. *Five great races*

permanent. They depend very slightly upon any mere external causes. They have, on the contrary, their foundation in some hidden principles connected with the origin of life, and with the mode of its transmission from parent to offspring, which the researches of philosophers have never yet been able to explore.

These same constitutional and congenital peculiarities which we see developing themselves all around us in families, mark, on a greater scale, the characteristics of the different nations of the earth, and in a degree much higher still, the several great and distinct races into which the whole human family seems to be divided. Physiologists consider that there are five of these great races, whose characteristics, mental as well as bodily, are distinctly, strongly, and permanently marked. These characteristics descend by hereditary succession from father to son, and though education and outward influences may modify them, they can not essentially change them. Compare, for example, the Indian and the African races, each of which has occupied for a thousand years a continent of its own, where they have been exposed to the same variety of climates, and as far as possible to the same general outward influences. How entirely diverse from each other they are, not only in form, color, and other physical marks, but in all the tendencies and characteristics of the soul! One can no more be changed into the other, than a wolf, by being tamed and domesticated, can be made a dog, or a dog, by being driven into the forests, be transformed into a tiger. The difference is still greater between either of these races and the Caucasian race. This race might probably be called the European race, were it not that some Asiatic and some African nations have sprung from it, as the Persians, the Phœnicians, the Egyptians, the Carthaginians, and, in modern times, the Turks. All the nations of this race, whether European or African, have been distinguished by the same physical marks in the conformation of the head and the color of the skin, and still more by those traits of character—the intellect, the energy, the spirit of determination and pride —which, far from owing their existence to outward circumstances, have always, in all ages, made all outward circumstances bend to them. That there have been some great and noble specimens of humanity among the African race, for example, no one can deny; but that there is a marked, and fixed, and permanent constitution al difference between them and the Caucasian race seems evident from this fact, that for two thousand years each has held its own continent, undisturbed, in a great degree, by the rest of mankind; and while, during all this time, no nation of the one race has risen, so far as is known, above the very lowest stage of civilization, there have been more than fifty entirely distinct and independent civilizations originated and fully developed in the other. For three thousand years the Caucasian race have continued, under all circumstances, and in every variety of situation, to exhibit the same traits and the same indomitable prowess. No calamities, however great—no desolating wars, no destructive pestilence, no wasting famine, no night of darkness, however universal and gloomy—has ever been able to keep them long in degradation or barbarism. There is not now a barbarous people to be found in the whole race, and there has not been one for a thousand years.

Nearly all the great exploits, and achievements too, which have signalized the history of the world, have been performed by this branch of the human family. They have given celebrity to every age in which they have lived, and to every country that they have ever possessed, by some great deed, or discovery, or achievement, which their intellectual energies have accomplished. As Egyptians, they built the Pyramids, and reared enormous monoliths, which remain as perfect now as they were when first completed, thirty centuries ago. As Phœnicians, they constructed ships, perfected navigation, and explored, without compass or chart, every known sea. As Greeks, they modeled architectural embellishments, and cut sculptures in marble, and wrote poems and history, which have been ever since the admiration of the world. As Romans, they carried a complete and perfect military organization over fifty nations and a hundred millions of people, with one supreme mistress over all, the ruins of whose splendid palaces and monuments have not yet passed away. Thus has this race gone on, always distinguishing itself, by energy, activity, and intellectual power, wherever it has dwelt, whatever language it has spoken, and in whatever period of the world it has lived. It has invented printing, and filled every country that it occupies with permanent records of the past, accessible to all. It has explored the heavens, and reduced to precise and exact calculations all the complicated motions there. It

Subordinate differences. — How accounted for

has ransacked the earth, systematized, arranged, and classified the vast melange of plants, and animals, and mineral products to be found upon its surface. It makes steam and falling water do more than half the work necessary for feeding and clothing the human race; and the howling winds of the ocean, the very emblems of resistless destruction and terror, it steadily employs in interchanging the products of the world, and bearing the means of comfort and plenty to every clime.

The Caucasian race has thus, in all ages, and in all the varieties of condition in which the different branches of it have been placed, evinced the same great characteristics, marking the existence of some innate and constant constitutional superiority; and yet, in the different branches, subordinate differences appear, which are to be accounted for, perhaps, partly by difference of circumstances, and partly, perhaps, by similar constitutional diversities—diversities by which one branch is distinguished from other branches, as the whole race is from the other races with which we have compared them. Among these branches, we, Anglo-Saxons ourselves, claim for the Anglo-Saxons the superiority over all the others

The Anglo-Saxons commenced their career as pirates and robbers, and as pirates and robbers of the most desperate and dangerous description. In fact, the character which the Anglo-Saxons have obtained in modern times for energy and enterprise, and for desperate daring in their conflicts with foes, is no recent fame. The progenitors of the present race were celebrated every where, and every where feared and dreaded, not only in the days of Alfred, but several centuries before. All the historians of those days that speak of them at all, describe them as universally distinguished above their neighbors for their energy and vehemence of character, their mental and physical superiority, and for the wild and daring expeditions to which their spirit of enterprise and activity were continually impelling them. They built vessels, in which they boldly put forth on the waters of the German Ocean or of the Baltic Sea on excursions for conquest or plunder. Like their present posterity on the British isles and on the shores of the Atlantic, they cared not, in these voyages, whether it was summer or winter, calm or storm. In fact, they sailed often in tempests and storms by choice, so as to come upon their enemies the more unexpectedly

SAXON MILITARY CHIEF

Courage and enterprise of the Anglo-Saxons. Their nautical exploits.

They would build small vessels, or rather boats, of osiers, covering them with skins, and in fleets of these frail floats they would sally forth among the howling winds and foaming surges of the German Ocean. On these expeditions, they all embarked as in a common cause, and felt a common interest. The leaders shared in all the toils and exposures of the men, and the men took part in the counsels and plans of the leaders. Their intelligence and activity, and their resistless courage and ardor, combined with their cool and calculating sagacity, made them successful in every attempt. If they fought, they conquered; if they pursued their enemies, they were sure to overtake them; if they retreated, they were sure to make their escape. They were clothed in a loose and flowing dress, and wore their hair long and hanging about their shoulders; and they had the art, as their descendants have now, of contriving and fabricating arms of such superior construction and workmanship, as to give them, on this account alone, a great advantage over all cotemporary nations. There were two other points in which there was a remarkable similarity between this parent stock in its rude, early form, and the extended social progeny which

represents it at the present day. One was the
extreme strictness of their ideas of conjugal
fidelity, and the stern and rigid severity with
which all violations of female virtue were judg-
ed. The woman who violated her marriage
vows was compelled to hang herself. Her body
was then burned in public, and the accomplice
of her crime was executed over the ashes. The
other point of resemblance between the ancient
Anglo-Saxons and their modern descendants
was their indomitable pride. They could never
endure any thing like *submission*. Though
sometimes overpowered, they were never conquered. Though taken prisoners and carried
captive, the indomitable spirit which animated
them could never be really subdued. The Romans used sometimes to compel their prisoners
to fight as gladiators, to make spectacles for
the amusement of the people of the city. On
one occasion, thirty Anglo-Saxons, who had
been taken captive and were reserved for this
fate, strangled themselves rather than submit
to this indignity. The whole nation manifested on all occasions a very unbending and un-
submissive will, encountering every possible
danger and braving every conceivable ill rather than succumb or submit to any power ex-

cept such as they had themselves created for their own ends; and their descendants, whether in England or America, evince much the same spirit still.

It was the landing of a few boat-loads of these determined and ferocious barbarians on a small island near the mouth of the Thames, which constitutes the great event of the arrival of the Anglo-Saxons in England, which is so celebrated in English history as the epoch which marks the real and true beginning of British greatness and power. It is true that the history of England goes back beyond this period to narrate, as we have done, the events connected with the contests of the Romans and the aboriginal Britons, and the incursions and maraudings of the Picts and Scots; but all these aborigines passed gradually—after the arrival of the Anglo-Saxons—off the stage. The old stock was wholly displaced. The present monarchy has sprung entirely from its Anglo-Saxon original; so that all which precedes the arrival of this new race is introductory and preliminary, like the history, in this country, of the native American tribes before the coming of the English Pilgrims. As, therefore, the landing of the Pilgrims on the Plymouth Rock marks the true commencement of the history of the American Republic, so ⸺ of the Anglo-Saxon adventurers on the island of Thanet represents and marks the origin of the British monarchy. The event, therefore, stands as a great and conspicuous landmark, though now dim and distant in the remote antiquity in which it occurred.

And yet the event, though so wide-reaching and grand in its bearings and relations, and in the vast consequences which have flowed and which still continue to flow from it, was apparently a minute and unimportant circumstance at the time when it occurred. There were only three vessels at the first arrival. Of their size and character the accounts vary. Some of these accounts say they contained three hundred men; others seem to state that the number which arrived at the first landing was three thousand. This, however, would seem impossible, as no three vessels built in those days could convey so large a number. We must suppose, therefore, that that number is meant to include those who came at several of the earlier expeditions, and which were grouped by the historian together, or else that several other vessels or transports accompanied the three.

which history has specially commemorated as the first arriving.

In fact, very little can now be known in respect to the form and capacity of the vessels in which these half-barbarous navigators roamed, in those days, over the British seas. Their name, indeed, has come down to us, and that is nearly all. They were called *cyules;* though the name is sometimes spelled, in the ancient chronicles, *ceols*, and in other ways. They were obviously vessels of considerable capacity and were of such construction and such strength as to stand the roughest marine exposures They were accustomed to brave fearlessly every commotion and to encounter every danger raised either by winter tempests or summer gales in the restless waters of the German Ocean.

The names of the commanders who headed the expedition which first landed have been preserved, and they have acquired, as might have been expected, a very wide celebrity. They were Hengist and Horsa. Hengist and Horsa were brothers.

The place where they landed was the island of Thanet. Thanet is a tract of land at the mouth of the Thames, on the southern side; a

The place of landing. — *The island of Thanet*

sort of promontory extending into the sea, and forming the cape at the south side of the estuary made by the mouth of the river. The extreme point of land is called the North Foreland which, as it is the point that thousands of vessels, coming out of the Thames, have to round in proceeding southward on voyages to France, to the Mediterranean, to the Indies, and to America, is very familiarly known to navigators throughout the world. The island of Thanet, of which this North Foreland is the extreme point, ought scarcely to be called an island, since it forms, in fact, a portion of the main land, being separated from it only by a narrow creek or stream, which in former ages indeed, was wide and navigable, but is now nearly choked up and obliterated by the sands and the sediment, which, after being brought down by the Thames, are driven into the creek by the surges of the sea.

In the time of Hengist and Horsa the creek was so considerable that its mouth furnished a sufficient harbor for their vessels. They landed at a town called Ebbs-fleet, which is now, however, at some distance inland.

There is some uncertainty in respect to the motive which led Hengist and Horsa to make their first descent upon the English coast. Whether they came on one of their customary piratical expeditions, or were driven on the coast accidentally by stress of weather, or were invited to come by the British king, can not now be accurately ascertained. Such parties of Anglo-Saxons had undoubtedly often landed before under somewhat similar circumstances and then, after brief incursions into the interior had re-embarked on board their ships and sailed away. In this case, however, there was a certain peculiar and extraordinary state of things in the political condition of the country in which they had landed, which resulted in first protracting their stay, and finally in establishing them so fixedly and permanently in the land, that they and their followers and descendants soon became the entire masters of it, and have remained in possession to the present day. These circumstances were as follows:

The name of the king of Britain at this period was Vortigern. At the time when the Anglo-Saxons arrived, he and his government were nearly overwhelmed with the pressure of difficulty and danger arising from the incursions of the Picts and Scots; and Vortigern, instead of being aroused to redoubled vigilance and energy

Character of Vortigern. He seeks the assistance of the Anglo-Saxons.

by the imminence of the danger, as Alfred afterward was in similar circumstances, sank down, as weak minds always do, in despair, and gave himself up to dissipation and vice—endeavoring, like depraved seamen on a wreck, to drown his mental distress in animal sensations of pleasure. Such men are ready to seek relief or rescue from their danger from any quarter and at any price. Vortigern, instead of looking upon the Anglo-Saxon intruders as new enemies, conceived the idea of appealing to them for succor. He offered to convey to them a large tract of territory in the part of the island where they had landed, on condition of their aiding him in his contests with his other foes.

Hengist and Horsa acceded to this proposal. They marched their followers into battle, and defeated Vortigern's enemies. They sent across the sea to their native land, and invited new adventurers to join them. Vortigern was greatly pleased with the success of his expedient. The Picts and Scots were driven back to their fastnesses in the remote mountains of the north, and the Britons once more possessed their land in peace, by means of the protection and the aid which their new confederates afforded them

In the mean time the Anglo-Saxons were establishing and strengthening themselves very rapidly in the part of the island which Vortigern had assigned them—which was, as the reader will understand from what has already been said in respect to the place of their landing, the southeastern part—a region which now constitutes the county of Kent. In addition, too, to the natural increase of their power from the increase of their numbers and their military force, Hengist contrived, if the story is true, to swell his own personal influence by means of a matrimonial alliance which he had the adroitness to effect. He had a daughter named Rowena. She was very beautiful and accomplished. Hengist sent for her to come to England When she had arrived he made a sumptuous entertainment for King Vortigern, inviting also to it, of course, many other distinguished guests. In the midst of the feast, when the king was in the state of high excitement produced on such temperaments by wine and convivial pleasure, Rowena came in to offer him more wine. Vortigern was powerfully struck, as Hengist had anticipated, with her grace and beauty. Learning that she was Hengist's daughter, he demanded her hand. Hengist at

Power of Hengist and Horsa.   Long contests.

first declined, but, after sufficiently stimulating the monarch's eagerness by his pretended opposition, he yielded, and the king became the general's son-in-law. This is the story which some of the old chroniclers tell. Modern historians are divided in respect to believing it. Some think it is fact, others fable.

At all events, the power of Hengist and Horsa gradually increased, as years passed on, until the Britons began to be alarmed at their growing strength and multiplying numbers, and to fear lest these new friends should prove, in the end, more formidable than the terrible enemies whom they had come to expel. Contentions and then open quarrels began to occur, and at length both parties prepared for war. The contest which soon ensued was a terrible struggle, or rather series of struggles, which continued for two centuries, during which the Anglo-Saxons were continually gaining ground and the Britons losing; the mental and physical superiority of the Anglo-Saxon race giving them, with very few exceptions, every where and always the victory.

There were, occasionally, intervals of peace, and partial and temporary friendliness. They accuse Hengist of great treachery on one of these occasions. He invited his son-in-law, King Vortigern, to a feast, with three hundred of his officers, and then fomenting a quarrel at the entertainment, the Britons were all killed in the affray by means of the superior Saxon force which had been provided for the emergency. Vortigern himself was taken prisoner, and held a captive until he ransomed himself by ceding three whole provinces to his captor. Hengist justified this demand by throwing the responsibility of the feud upon his guests; and it is not, in fact, at all improbable that they deserved their share of the condemnation.

The famous King Arthur, whose Knights of the Round Table have been so celebrated in ballads and tales, lived and flourished during these wars between the Saxons and the Britons. He was a king of the Britons, and performed wonderful exploits of strength and valor. He was of prodigious size and muscular power, and of undaunted bravery. He slew giants, destroyed the most ferocious wild beasts, gained very splendid victories in the battles that he fought, made long expeditions into foreign countries, having once gone on a pilgrimage to Jerusalem to obtain the Holy Cross. His wife was a beautiful lady, the daughter of a chieftain of Cornwall. Her name was Guenever.* On his return from one of his distant expeditions, he found that his nephew, Medrawd, had won her affections while he was gone, and a combat ensued in consequence between him and Medrawd. The combat took place on the coast of Cornwall. Both parties fell. Arthur was mortally wounded. They took him from the field into a boat, and carried him along the coast till they came to a river. They ascended the river till they came to the town of Glastonbury. They committed the still breathing body to the care of faithful friends there; but the mortal blow had been given. The great hero died, and they buried his body in the Glastonbury churchyard, very deep beneath the surface of the ground, in order to place it as effectually as possible beyond the reach of Saxon rage and vengeance. Arthur had been a deadly and implacable foe to the Saxons. He had fought twelve great pitched battles with them, in every one of which he had gained the victory In one of these battles he had slain, according to the traditional tale, four hundred and seventy men, in one day, with his own hand.

Five hundred years after his death, King

---

* Spelled sometimes Gwenlyfar and Ginevra

King Arthur's grave.   *Disinterment of his body.*

Henry the Second, having heard from an ancient British bard that Arthur's body lay interred in the Abbey of Glastonbury, and that the spot was marked by some small pyramids erected near it, and that the body would be found in a rude coffin made of a hollowed oak, ordered search to be made. The ballads and tales which had been then, for several centuries, circulating throughout England, narrating and praising King Arthur's exploits, had given him so wide a fame, that great interest was felt in the recovery and the identification of his remains. The searchers found the pyramids in the cemetery of the abbey. They dug between them, and came at length to a stone. Beneath this stone was a leaden cross, with the inscription in Latin, "HERE LIES BURIED THE BODY OF GREAT KING ARTHUR." Going down still below this, they came at length, at the depth of sixteen feet from the surface, to a great coffin, made of the trunk of an oak tree, and within it was a human skeleton of unusual size. The skull was very large, and showed marks of ten wounds. Nine of them were closed by concretions of the bone, indicating that the wounds by which those contusions or fractures had been made had been healed while life continued

The tenth fracture remained in a condition which showed that that had been the mortal wound.

The bones of Arthur's wife were found near those of her husband. The hair was apparently perfect when found, having all the freshness and beauty of life; but a monk of the abbey, who was present at the disinterment, touched it and it crumbled to dust.

Such are the tales which the old chronicles tell of the good King Arthur, the last and greatest representative of the power of the ancient British aborigines. It is a curious illustration of the uncertainty which attends all the early records of national history, that, notwithstanding all the above particularity respecting the life and death of Arthur, it is a serious matter of dispute among the learned in modern times whether any such person ever lived.

Final subjugation of the Britons. The Saxon Heptarchy

Chapter III.
The Danes.

THE landing of Hengist and Horsa, the first of the Anglo-Saxons, took place in the year 449, according to the commonly received chronology. It was more than two hundred years after this before the Britons were entirely subdued, and the Saxon authority established throughout the island, unquestioned and supreme. One or two centuries more passed away, and then the Anglo-Saxons had, in their turn, to resist a new horde of invaders, who came, as they themselves had done, across the German Ocean. These new invaders were the Danes.

The Saxons were not united under one general government when they came finally to get settled in their civil polity. The English territory was divided, on the contrary, into seven or eight separate kingdoms. These kingdoms were ruled by as many separate dynasties, or lines of kings. They were connected with each other by friendly relations and alliances, more or less intimate, the whole system being known in history by the name of the Saxon Heptarchy

The princes of these various dynasties showed in their dealings with one another, and in their relations with foreign powers, the same characteristics of boldness and energy as had always marked the action of the race. Even the queens and princesses evinced, by their courage and decision, that Anglo-Saxon blood lost nothing of its inherent qualities by flowing in female veins.

For example, a very extraordinary story is told of one of these Saxon princesses. A certain king upon the Continent, whose dominions lay between the Rhine and the German Ocean, had proposed for her hand in behalf of his son, whose name was Radiger. The consent of the princess was given, and the contract closed. The king himself soon afterward died, but before he died he changed his mind in respect to the marriage of his son. It seems that he had himself married a second wife, the daughter of a king of the Franks, a powerful continental people; and as, in consequence of his own approaching death, his son would come unexpectedly into possession of the throne, and would need immediately all the support which a pow-

Faithlessness of Radiger.   *Indignation of the princess*

erful alliance could give him, he recommended to him to give up the Saxon princess, and connect himself, instead, with the Franks, as he himself had done. The prince entered into these views; his father died, and he immediately afterward married his father's youthful widow—his own step-mother—a union which, however monstrous it would be regarded in our day, seems not to have been considered any thing very extraordinary then.

The Anglo-Saxon princess was very indignant at this violation of his plighted faith on the part of her suitor. She raised an army and equipped a fleet, and set sail with the force which she had thus assembled across the German Ocean, to call the faithless Radiger to account. Her fleet entered the mouth of the Rhine, and her troops landed, herself at the head of them. She then divided her army into two portions, keeping one division as a guard for herself at her own encampment, which she established near the place of her landing, while she sent the other portion to seek and attack Radiger, who was, in the mean time, assembling his forces, in a state of great alarm at this sudden and unexpected danger.

In due time this division returned, reporting

Radiger a prisoner. *He marries the princess.*

that they had met and encountered Radiger,
and had entirely defeated him. They came
back triumphing in their victory, considering
evidently, that the faithless lover had been well
punished for his offense. The princess, however, instead of sharing in their satisfaction,
ordered them to make a new incursion into the
interior, and not to return without bringing
Radiger with them as their prisoner. They
did so; and after hunting the defeated and distressed king from place to place, they succeeded, at last, in seizing him in a wood, and
brought him in to the princess's encampment.
He began to plead for his life, and to make excuses for the violation of his contract by urging
the necessities of his situation and his father's
dying commands. The princess said she was
ready to forgive him if he would now dismiss
her rival and fulfill his obligations to her. Radiger yielded to this demand; he repudiated his
Frank wife, and married the Anglo-Saxon lady
in her stead.

Though the Anglo-Saxon race continued thus
to evince in all their transactions the same extraordinary spirit and energy, and met generally with the same success that had characterized them at the beginning, they seemed at

The Danes.	Their habits and character

length to find their equals in the Danes. These Danes, however, though generally designated by that appellation in history, were not exclusively the natives of Denmark. They came from all the shores of the Northern and Baltic Seas. In fact, they inhabited the sea rather than the land. They were a race of bold and fierce naval adventurers, as the Anglo-Saxons themselves had been two centuries before. Most extraordinary accounts are given of their hardihood, and of their fierce and predatory habits. They haunted the bays along the coasts of Sweden and Norway, and the islands which encumber the entrance to the Baltic Sea. They were banded together in great hordes, each ruled by a chieftain, who was called a *sea king*, because his dominions scarcely extended at all to the land. His possessions, his power, his subjects pertained all to the sea. It is true they built or bought their vessels on the shore, and they sought shelter among the islands and in the bays in tempests and storms; but they prided themselves in never dwelling in houses or sharing, in any way, the comforts or enjoyments of the land. They made excursions every where for conquest and plunder, and were proud of their successful deeds of violence and wrong. It was honorable to enter into their service. Chieftains and nobles who dwelt upon the land sent their sons to acquire greatness, and wealth, and fame by joining these piratical gangs, just as high-minded military or naval officers, in modern times, would enter into the service of an honorable government abroad.

Besides the great leaders of the most powerful of these bands, there was an infinite number of petty chieftains, who commanded single ships or small detached squadrons. These were generally the younger sons of sovereigns or chieftains who lived upon the land, the elder brothers remaining at home to inherit the throne or the paternal inheritance. It was discreditable then, as it is now in Europe, for any branches of families of the higher class to engage in any pursuit of honorable industry They could plunder and kill without dishonor, but they could not toil. To rob and murder was glory; to do good or to be useful in any way was disgrace.

These younger sons went to sea at a very early age too. They were sent often at twelve, that they might become early habituated to the exposures and dangers of their dreadful combats, and of the wintery storms, and inured to

| Piratical excursions. | Booty and spoil. |

the athletic exertions which the sea rigorously exacts of all who venture within her dominion. When they returned they were received with consideration and honor, or with neglect and disgrace, according as they were more or less laden with booty and spoil. In the summer months the land kings themselves would organize and equip naval armaments for similar expeditions. They would cruise along the coasts of the sea, to land where they found an unguarded point, and sack a town or burn a castle, seize treasures, capture men and make them slaves, kidnap women, and sometimes destroy helpless children with their spears in a manner too barbarous and horrid to be described. On returning to their homes, they would perhaps find their own castles burned and their own dwellings roofless, from the visit of some similar horde.

Thus the seas of western Europe were covered in those days, as they are now, with fleets of shipping; though, instead of being engaged as now, in the quiet and peaceful pursuits of commerce, freighted with merchandise, manned with harmless seamen, and welcome wherever they come, they were then loaded only with ammunition and arms, and crowded with fierce and reckless robbers, the objects of universal detestation and terror.

One of the first of these sea kings who acquired sufficient individual distinction to be personally remembered in history has given a sort of immortality, by his exploits, to the very rude name of Ragnar Lodbrog, and his character was as rude as his name.

Ragnar's father was a prince of Norway. He married, however, a Danish princess, and thus Ragnar acquired a sort of hereditary right to a Danish kingdom—the territory including various islands and promontories at the entrance of the Baltic Sea. There was, however, a competitor for this power, named Harald. The Franks made common cause with Harald. Ragnar was defeated and driven away from the land. Though defeated, however, he was not subdued. He organized a naval force, and made himself a sea king. His operations on the stormy element of the seas were conducted with so much decision and energy, and at the same time with so much system and plan, that his power rapidly extended. He brought the other sea kings under his control, and established quite a maritime empire. He made more and more distant excursions, and at last, in or-

| Ragnar invades France. | Incursions into Spain. |

der to avenge himself upon the Franks for their interposition in behalf of his enemy at home, he passed through the Straits of Dover, and thence down the English Channel to the mouth of the Seine. He ascended this river to Rouen, and there landed, spreading throughout the country the utmost terror and dismay. From Rouen he marched to Paris, finding no force able to resist him on his way, or to defend the capital. His troops destroyed the monastery of St. Germain's, near the city, and then the King of the Franks, finding himself at their mercy, bought them off by paying a large sum of money. With this money and the other booty which they had acquired, Ragnar and his horde now returned to their ships at Rouen, and sailed away again toward their usual haunts among the bays and islands of the Baltic Sea.

This exploit, of course, gave Ragnar Lodbrog's barbarous name a very wide celebrity. It tended, too, greatly to increase and establish his power. He afterward made similar incursions into Spain, and finally grew bold enough to brave the Anglo-Saxons themselves on the green island of Britain, as the Anglo-Saxons had themselves braved the aboriginal inhabitants two or three centuries before. But Ragnar seems to have found the Anglo-Saxon swords and spears which he advanced to encounter on landing in England much more formidable than those which were raised against him on the southern side of the Channel. He was destroyed in the contest. The circumstances were as follows:

In making his preparations for a descent upon the English coast, he prepared for a very determined contest, knowing well the character of the foes with whom he would have now to deal. He built two enormous ships, much larger than those of the ordinary size, and armed and equipped them in the most perfect manner. He filled them with selected men, and sailing down along the coast of Scotland, he watched for a place and an opportunity to land. Winds and storms are almost always raging among the dark and gloomy mountains and islands of Scotland. Ragnar's ships were caught in one of these gales and driven on shore. The ships were lost, but the men escaped to the land. Ragnar, nothing daunted, organized and marshaled them as an army, and marched into the interior to attack any force which might appear against them. His course led him to Northumbria, the most northerly Saxon king-

[A.D. 850.] THE DANES.

Ragnar defeated by the Saxons. *His cruel death.*

don. Here he soon encountered a very large and superior force, under the command of Ella, the king; but, with the reckless desperation which so strongly marked his character, he advanced to attack them. Three times, it is said, he pierced the enemy's lines, cutting his way entirely through them with his little column. He was, however, at length overpowered. His men were cut to pieces, and he was himself taken prisoner. We regret to have to add that our cruel ancestors put their captive to death in a very barbarous manner. They filled a den with poisonous snakes, and then drove the wretched Ragnar into it. The horrid reptiles killed him with their stings. It was Ella, the king of Northumbria, who ordered and directed this punishment.

The expedition of Ragnar thus ended without leading to any permanent results in Anglo-Saxon history. It is, however, memorable as the first of a series of invasions from the Danes —or Northmen, as they are sometimes called, since they came from all the coasts of the Baltic and German Seas—which, in the end, gave the Anglo-Saxons infinite trouble. At one time, in fact, the conquests of the Danes threatened to root out and destroy the Anglo-Saxon power from the island altogether. They would probably have actually effected this, had the nation not been saved by the prudence, the courage, the sagacity, and the consummate skill of the subject of this history, as will fully appear to the reader in the course of future chapters.

Ragnar was not the only one of these Northmen who made attempts to land in England and to plunder the Anglo-Saxons, even in his own day. Although there were no very regular historical records kept in those early times, still a great number of legends, and ballads, and ancient chronicles have come down to us, narrating the various transactions which occurred, and it appears by these that the sea kings generally were beginning, at this time, to harass the English coasts, as well as all the other shores to which they could gain access. Some of these invasions would seem to have been of a very formidable character.

At first these excursions were made in the summer season only, and, after collecting their plunder, the marauders would return in the autumn to their own shores, and winter in the bays and among the islands there. At length, nowever, they grew more bold. A large band of them landed, in the autumn of 851, on the island of Thanet, where the Saxons themselves had landed four centuries before, and began very coolly to establish their winter quarters on English ground. They succeeded in maintaining their stay during the winter, and in the spring were prepared for bolder undertakings still.

They formed a grand confederation, and collected a fleet of three hundred and fifty ships, galleys, and boats, and advanced boldly up the Thames. They plundered London, and then marched south to Canterbury, which they plundered too. They went thence into one of the Anglo Saxon kingdoms called Mercia, the inhabitants of the country not being able to oppose any effectual obstacle to their marauding march. Finally, a great Anglo-Saxon force was organized and brought out to meet them. The battle was fought in a forest of oaks, and the Danes were defeated. The victory, however, afforded the Anglo-Saxon kingdoms only a temporary relief. New hordes were continually arriving and landing, growing more and more bold if they met with success, and but little daunted or discouraged by temporary failures.

The most formidable of all these expeditions

The sons and relatives of Ragnar.   *Their plans and preparations.*

was one organized and commanded by the sons and relatives of Ragnar, whom, it will be recollected, the Saxons had cruelly killed by poisonous serpents in a dungeon or den. The relatives of the unhappy chieftain thus barbarously executed were animated in their enterprise by the double stimulus of love of plunder and a ferocious thirst for revenge. A considerable time was spent in collecting a large fleet, and in combining, for this purpose, as many chieftains as could be induced to share in the enterprise. The story of their fellow-countryman expiring under the stings of adders and scorpions, while his tormentors were exulting around him over the cruel agonies which their ingenuity had devised, aroused them to a phrensy of hatred and revenge. They proceeded, however, very deliberately in their plans. They did nothing hastily. They allowed ample time for the assembling and organizing of the confederation. When all was ready, they found that there were eight kings and twenty earls in the alliance, generally the relatives and comrades of Ragnar. The two most prominent of these commanders were Guthrum and Hubba. Hubba was one of Ragnar's sons. At length, toward the close of the summer, the formidable

| The Danes winter in England. | Alarm of the Saxons. |

expedition set sail. They approached the English coast, and landed without meeting with any resistance. The Saxons seemed appalled and paralyzed at the greatness of the danger. The several kingdoms of the Heptarchy, though they had been imperfectly united, some years before, under Egbert, were still more or less distinct, and each hoped that the one first invaded would be the only one which would suffer; and as these kingdoms were rivals, and often hostile to each other, no general league was formed against what soon proved to be the common enemy. The Danes, accordingly, quietly encamped, and made calm and deliberate arrangements for spending the winter in their new quarters, as if they were at home.

During all this time, notwithstanding the coolness and deliberation with which these avengers of their murdered countryman acted, the fires of their resentment and revenge were slowly but steadily burning, and as soon as the spring opened, they put themselves in battle array, and marched into the dominions of Ella. Ella did all that it was possible to do to meet and oppose them, but the spirit of retaliation and rage which his cruelties had evoked was too strong to be resisted. His country was rav aged, his army was defeated, he was taken prisoner, and the dying terrors and agonies of Ragnar among the serpents were expiated by tenfold worse tortures which they inflicted upon Ella's mutilated body, by a process too horrible to be described.

After thus successfully accomplishing the great object of their expedition, it was to have been hoped that they would leave the island and return to their Danish homes. But they evinced no disposition to do this. On the contrary, they commenced a course of ravage and conquest in all parts of England, which continued for several years. The parts of the country which attempted to oppose them they destroyed by fire and sword. They seized cities, garrisoned and occupied them, and settled in them as if to make them their permanent homes. One kingdom after another was subdued. The kingdom of Wessex seemed alone to remain, and that was the subject of contest. Ethelred was the king. The Danes advanced into his dominions to attack him. In the battle that ensued, Ethelred was killed. The successor to his throne was his brother Alfred, the subject of this history, who thus found himself suddenly and unexpectedly called upon to assume the responsibilities and powers of supreme command, in as dark and trying a crisis of national calamity and danger as can well be conceived. The manner in which Alfred acted in the emergency, rescuing his country from her perils, and laying the foundations, as he did, of all the greatness and glory which has since accrued to her, has caused his memory to be held in the highest estimation among all nations, and has immortalized his name.

Chapter IV

Alfred's Early Years.

BEFORE commencing the narrative of Alfred's administration of the public affairs of his realm, it is necessary to go back a little, in order to give some account of the more private occurrences of his early life. Alfred, like Washington, was distinguished for a very extraordinary combination of qualities which exhibited itself in his character, viz., the combination of great military energy and skill on the one hand, with a very high degree, on the other, of moral and religious principle, and conscientious devotion to the obligations of duty. This combination, so rarely found in the distinguished personages which have figured among mankind, is, in a great measure, explained and accounted for, in Alfred's case, by the peculiar circumstances of his early history.

It was his brother Ethelred, as has already been stated, whom Alfred immediately succeeded His father's name was Ethelwolf; and it seems highly probable that the peculiar turn which Alfred's mind seemed to take in after

Alfred's father, Ethelwolf. *Monasteries*

years, was the consequence, in some considerable degree, of this parent's situation and character. Ethelwolf was a younger son, and was brought up in a monastery at Winchester. The monasteries of those days were the seats ooth of learning and piety, that is, of such learning and piety as then prevailed. The ideas of religious faith and duty which were entertained a thousand years ago were certainly very different from those which are received now; still, there was then, mingled with much superstition, a great deal of honest and conscientious devotion to the principles of Christian duty, and of sincere and earnest desire to live for the honor of God and religion, and for the highest and best welfare of mankind. Monastic establishments existed every where, defended by the sacredness which invested them from the storms of violence and war which swept over every thing which the cross did not protect. To these the thoughtful, the serious, and the intellectual retired, leaving the restless, the rude, and the turbulent to distract and terrify the earth with their endless quarrels. Here they studied, they wrote, they read; they transcribed books, they kept records, they arranged exercises of devotion, they educated youth, and, in a word, per

Ethelwolf retires to a monastery.   He is released from his vows

formed, in the inclosed and secluded retreats in which they sought shelter, those intellectual functions of civil life which now can all be performed in open exposure, but which in those days, if there had been no monastic retreats to shelter them, could not have been performed at all. For the learning and piety of the present age, whether Catholic or Protestant, to malign the monasteries of Anglo-Saxon times is for the oak to traduce the acorn from which it sprung.

Ethelwolf was a younger son, and, consequently, did not expect to reign. He went to the monastery at Winchester, and took the vows. His father had no objection to this plan, satisfied with having his oldest son expect and prepare for the throne. As, however, he advanced toward manhood, the thought of the probability that he might be called to the throne in the event of his brother's death led all parties to desire that he might be released from his monastic vows. They applied, accordingly, to the pope for a dispensation. The dispensation was granted, and Ethelwolf became a general in the army. In the end his brother died, and he became king.

He continued, however, during his reign, to manifest the peaceful, quiet, and serious character which had led him to enter the monastery, and which had probably been strengthened and confirmed by the influences and habits to which he had been accustomed there. He had, however, a very able, energetic, and warlike minister, who managed his affairs with great ability and success for a long course of years. Ethelwolf, in the mean time, leaving public affairs to his minister, continued to devote himself to the pursuits to which his predilections inclined him. He visited monasteries he cultivated learning; he endowed the Church; he made journeys to Rome. All this time, his kingdom, which had before almost swallowed up the other kingdoms of the Heptarchy, became more and more firmly established, until, at length, the Danes came in, as is described in the last chapter, and brought the whole land into the most extreme and imminent danger. The case did not, however, become absolutely desperate until after Ethelwolf's death, as will be hereafter explained.

Ethelwolf married a lady whose gentle, quiet, and serious character corresponded with his own. Alfred was the youngest, and, as is often the case with the youngest, the favorite child He was kept near to his father and mother, and closely under their influence, until his mother died, which event, however, took place when he was quite young. After this, Ethelwolf sent Alfred to Rome. Rome was still more the great center then than it is now of religion and learning. There were schools there, maintained by the various nations of Europe respectively, for the education of the sons of the nobility. Alfred, however, did not go for this purpose. It was only to make the journey, to see the city, to be introduced to the pope, and to be presented, by means of the fame of the expedition, to the notice of Europe, as the future sovereign of England; for it was Ethelwolf's intention, at this time, to pass over his older sons, and make this Benjamin his successor on the throne.

The journey was made with great pomp and parade. A large train of nobles and ecclesiastics accompanied the young prince, and a splendid reception was given to him in the various towns in France which he passed through on his way. He was but five years old; but his position and his prospects made him, though so young, a personage of great distinction. After spending a short time at Rome, he returned again to England.

Ethelwolf goes to Rome.   Arrangements for the journey

Two years after this, Ethelwolf, Alfred's father, determined to go to Rome himself. His wife had died, his older sons had grown up, and his own natural aversion to the cares and toils of government seems to have been increased by the alarms and dangers produced by the incursions of the Danes, and by his own advancing years. Having accordingly arranged the affairs of the kingdom by placing his oldest sons in command, he took the youngest, Alfred, who was now seven years old, with him, and, crossing the Channel, landed on the Continent, on his way to Rome.

All the arrangements for this journey were conducted on a scale of great magnificence and splendor. It is true that it was a rude and semi-barbarous age, and very little progress had been made in respect to the peaceful and industrial arts of life; but, in respect to the arts connected with war, to every thing that related to the march of armies, the pomp and parade of royal progresses, the caparison of horses, the armor and military dresses of men, and the parade and pageantry of military spectacles, a very considerable degree of advancement had been attained.

King Ethelwolf availed himself of all the resources that he could command to give eclat to his journey. He had a numerous train of attendants and followers, and he carried with him a number of rich and valuable presents for the pope. He was received with great distinction by King Charles of France, through whose dominions he had to pass on his way to Italy Charles had a daughter, Judith, a young girl with whom Ethelwolf, though now himself quite advanced in life, fell deeply in love.

Ethelwolf, after a short stay in France, went on to Rome. His arrival and his visit here attracted great attention. As King of England he was a personage of very considerable consequence, and then he came with a large retinue and in magnificent state. His religious predilections, too, inspired him with a very strong interest in the ecclesiastical authorities and institutions of Rome, and awakened, reciprocally in these authorities, a strong interest in him He made costly presents to the pope, some of which were peculiarly splendid. One was a crown of pure gold, which weighed, it is said, four pounds. Another was a sword, richly mounted in gold. There were also several utensils and vessels of Saxon form and construction, some of gold and others of silver gilt, and also a

Distribution of money. **Ethelwolf's resources**

considerable number of dresses, all very richly adorned. King Ethelwolf also made a distribution in money to all the inhabitants of Rome: gold to the nobles and to the clergy, and silver to the people. How far his munificence on this occasion may have been exaggerated by the Saxon chroniclers, who, of course, like other early historians, were fond of magnifying all the exploits, and swelling, in every way, the fame of the heroes of their stories, we can not now know. There is no doubt, however, that all the circumstances of Ethelwolf's visit to the great capital were such as to attract universal attention to the event, and to make the little Alfred, on whose account the journey was in a great measure performed, an object of very general interest and attention.

In fact, there is every reason to believe that the Saxon nations had, at that time, made such progress in wealth, population, and power as to afford to such a prince as Ethelwolf the means of making a great display, if he chose to do so, on such an occasion as that of a royal progress through France and a visit to the great city of Rome. The Saxons had been in possession of England, at this time, many hundred years; and though, during all this period, they had been involved in various wars, both with one another and with the neighboring nations, they had been all the time steadily increasing in wealth, and making constant improvements in all the arts and refinements of life. Ethelwolf reigned, therefore, over a people of considerable wealth and power, and he moved across the Continent on his way to Rome, and figured while there, as a personage of no ordinary distinction.

Rome was at this time, as we have said, the great center of education, as well as of religious and ecclesiastical influence. In fact, education and religion went hand in hand in those days, there being scarcely any instruction in books excepting for the purposes of the Church. Separate schools had been established at Rome by the leading nations of Europe, where their youth could be taught, each at an institution in which his own language was spoken. Ethelwolf remained a year at Rome, to give Alfred the benefit of the advantages which the city afforded. The boy was of a reflective and thoughtful turn of mind, and applied himself diligently to the performance of his duties. His mind was rapidly expanded, his powers were developed, and stores of such knowledge as was adapted to the circumstances and wants of the

| The Saxon seminary burned. | Rebuilt by Ethelwolf |

times were laid up. The religious and intellectual influences thus brought to bear upon the young Alfred's mind produced strong and decided effects in the formation of his character —effects which were very strikingly visible in his subsequent career.

Ethelwolf found, when he arrived at Rome, that the Saxon seminary had been burned the preceding year. It had been founded by a former Saxon king. Ethelwolf rebuilt it, and placed the institution on a new and firmer foundation than before. He also obtained some edicts from the papal government to secure and confirm certain rights of his Saxon subjects residing in the city, which rights had, it seems, been in some degree infringed upon, and he thus saved his subjects from oppressions to which they had been exposed. In a word, Ethelwolf's visit not only afforded an imposing spectacle to those who witnessed the pageantry and the ceremonies which marked it, but it was attended with permanent and substantial benefits to many classes, who became, in consequence of it, the objects of the pious monarch's benevolent regard.

At length, when the year had expired, Ethelwolf set out on his return He went back

Ethelwolf in France.   *He falls in love with Judith.*

through France, as he came, and during his stay in that country on the way home, an event occurred which was of no inconsiderable consequence to Alfred himself, and which changed or modified Ethelwolf's whole destiny. The event was that, having, as before stated, become enamored with the young Princess Judith, the daughter of the King of France, Ethelwolf demanded her in marriage. We have no means of knowing how the proposal affected the princess herself; marriages in that rank and station in life were then, as they are now in fact, wholly determined and controlled by great political considerations, or by the personal predilections of powerful *men*, with very little regard for the opinions or desires of the party whose happiness was most to be affected by the result. At all events, whatever may have been Judith's opinion, the marriage was decided upon and consummated, and the venerable king returned to England with his youthful bride The historians of the day say, what would seem almost incredible, that she was but about twelve years old.

Judith's Saxon name was Leotheta. She made an excellent mother to the young Alfred, though she innocently and indirectly caused her

Ethelwolf's death. *Ethelbald.*

husband much trouble in his realm. Alfred's older brothers were wild and turbulent men, and one of them, Ethelbald, was disposed to retain a portion of the power with which he had been invested during his father's absence, instead of giving it up peaceably on his return. He organized a rebellion against his father, making the king's course of conduct in respect to his youthful bride the pretext. Ethelwolf was very fond of his young wife, and seemed disposed to elevate her to a position of great political consideration and honor. Ethelbald complained of this. The father, loving peace rather than war, compromised the question with him, and relinquished to him a part of his kingdom. Two years after this he died, leaving Ethelbald the entire possession of the throne. Ethelbald, as if to complete and consummate his unnatural conduct toward his father, persuaded the beautiful Judith, his father's widow, to become his wife, in violation not only of all laws human and divine, but also of those universal instincts of propriety which no lapse of time and no changes of condition can eradicate from the human soul. This second union throws some light on the question of Judith's action. Since she was willing to marry her husband's son to *preserve* the position of a queen, we may well suppose that she did not object to uniting herself to the father in order to attain it. Perhaps, however, we ought to consider that no responsibility whatever, in transactions of this character, should attach to such a mere child.

During all this time Alfred was passing from his eighth to his twelfth year. He was a very intelligent and observing boy, and had acquired much knowledge of the world and a great deal of general information in the journeys which he had taken with his father, both about England and also on the Continent, in France and Italy. Judith had taken a great interest in his progress. She talked with him, she encouraged his inquiries, she explained to him what he did not understand, and endeavored in every way to develop and strengthen his mental powers. Alfred was a favorite, and, as such, was always very much indulged; but there was a certain conscientiousness and gentleness of spirit which marked his character even in these early years, and seemed to defend him from the injurious influences which indulgence and extreme attention and care often produce. Alfred was considerate, quiet, and reflective; he improved the

Alfred's fondness for Anglo-Saxon poetry. — Its character

privileges which he enjoyed, and did not abuse the kindness and the favors which every one by whom he was known lavished upon him.

Alfred was very fond of the Anglo-Saxon poetry which abounded in those days. The poems were legends, ballads, and tales, which described the exploits of heroes, and the adventures of pilgrims and wanderers of all kinds. These poems were to Alfred what Homer's poems were to Alexander. He loved to listen to them, to hear them recited, and to commit them to memory. In committing them to memory, he was obliged to depend upon hearing the poems repeated by others, for he himself could not read.

And yet he was now twelve years old. It may surprise the reader, perhaps, to be thus told, after all that has been said of the attention paid to Alfred's education, and of the progress which he had made, that he could not even read. But reading, far from being then considered, as it is now, an essential attainment for all, and one which we are sure of finding possessed by all who have received any instruction whatever, was regarded in those days a sort of technical art, learned only by those who were to make some professional use of the acquisition. Monks and clerks could always read, but generals, gentlemen, and kings very seldom. And as they could not read, neither could they write. They made a rude cross at the end of the writings which they wished to authenticate instead of signing their names—a mode which remains to the present day, though it has descended to the very lowest and humblest classes of society.

In fact, even the upper classes of society could not generally learn to read in those days, for there were no books. Every thing recorded was in manuscripts, the characters being written with great labor and care, usually on parchment, the captions and leading letters being often splendidly illuminated and adorned by gilded miniatures of heads, or figures, or landscapes, which enveloped or surrounded them Judith had such a manuscript of some Saxon poems. She had learned the language while in France. One day Alfred was looking at the book, and admiring the character in which it was written, particularly the ornamented letters at the headings. Some of his brothers were in the room, they, of course, being much older than he Judith said that either of them might have the book who would first learn to read it. The older brothers paid little attention to this

Alfred desires to learn Latin.   *Latin literature.*

proposal, but Alfred's interest was strongly awakened. He immediately sought and found some one to teach him, and before long he read the volume to Judith, and claimed it as his own. She rejoiced at his success, and fulfilled her promise with the greatest pleasure.

Alfred soon acquired, by his Anglo-Saxon studies, a great taste for books, and had next a strong desire to study the Latin language. The scholars of the various nations of Europe formed at that time, as, in fact, they do now, one community, linked together by many ties. They wrote and spoke the Latin language, that being the only language which could be understood by them all. In fact, the works which were most highly valued then by the educated men of all nations, were the poems and the histories, and other writings produced by the classic authors of the Roman commonwealth. There were also many works on theology, on ecclesiastical polity, and on law, of great authority and in high repute, all written in the Latin tongue. Copies of these works were made by the monks, in their retreats in abbeys and monasteries, and learned men spent their lives in perusing them. To explore this field was not properly a duty incumbent upon a young prince destined to take a seat upon a throne, but Alfred felt a great desire to undertake the work. He did not do it, however, for the reason, as he afterward stated, that there was no one at court at the time who was qualified to teach him.

Alfred, though he had thus--the thoughtful and reflective habits of a student, was also active, and graceful, and strong in his bodily development. He excelled in all the athletic recreations of the time, and was especially famous for his skill, and courage, and power as a hunter. He gave every indication, in a word, at this early age, of possessing that uncommon combination of mental and personal qualities which fits those who possess it to secure and maintain a great ascendency among mankind.

The unnatural union which had been formed on the death of Ethelwolf between his youthful widow and her aged husband's son did not long continue. The people of England were very much shocked at such a marriage, and a great prelate, the Bishop of Winchester, remonstrated against it with such sternness and authority, that Ethelbald not only soon put his wife away, but submitted to a severe penance which the bishop imposed upon him in retribution for his sin. Judith, thus forsaken, soon afterward sold

Judith returns to her native land.   *She marries a third time.*

the lands and estates which her two husbands had severally granted her, and, taking a final leave of Alfred, whom she tenderly loved, she returned to her native land. Not long after this, she was married a third time, to a continental prince, whose dominions lay between the Baltic and the Rhine, and from this period she disappears entirely from the stage of Alfred's history

Chapter V.

State of England.

HAVING thus brought down the narrative of Alfred's early life as far and as fully as the records that remain enable us to do so, we resume the general history of the national affairs by returning to the subject of the depredations and conquests of the Danes, and the circumstances connected with Alfred's accession to the throne.

To give the reader some definite and clear ideas of the nature of this warfare, it will be well to describe in detail some few of the incidents and scenes which ancient historians have recorded. The following was one case which occurred:

The Danes, it must be premised, were particularly hostile to the monasteries and religious establishments of the Anglo-Saxons. In the first place, they were themselves pagans, and they hated Christianity. In the second place, they knew that these places of sacred seclusion were often the depositories selected for the custody or concealment of treasure; and, besides

Plunderings of the Danes. *Their cruelties to monks and nuns*

the treasures which kings and potentates often placed in them for safety, these establishments possessed utensils of gold and silver for the service of the chapels, and a great variety of valuable gifts, such as pious saints or penitent sinners were continually bequeathing to them The Danes were, consequently, never better pleased than when sacking an abbey or a monastery. In such exploits they gratified their terrible animal propensities, both of hatred and love, by the cruelties which they perpetrated personally upon the monks and the nuns, and at the same time enriched their coffers with the most valuable spoils. A dreadful tale is told of one company of nuns, who, in the consternation and terror which they endured at the approach of a band of Danes, mutilated their faces in a manner too horrid to be described, as the only means left to them for protection against the brutality of their foes. They followed, in adopting this measure, the advice and the example of the lady superior. It was effectual.

There was a certain abbey, called Crowland, which was in those days one of the most celebrated in the island. It was situated near the southern border of Lincolnshire, which lies on the eastern side of England. There is a great

Abbey of Crowland. *Its ruins still remain.*

shallow bay, called The Wash, on this eastern shore, and it is surrounded by a broad tract of low and marshy land, which is drained by long canals, and traversed by roads built upon embankments. Dikes skirt the margins of the streams, and wind-mills are engaged in perpetual toil to raise the water from the fields into the channels by which it is conveyed away.

Crowland is at the confluence of two rivers, which flow sluggishly through this flat but beautiful and verdant region. The remains of the old abbey still stand, built on piles driven into the marshy ground, and they form at the present time a very interesting mass of ruins The year before Alfred acceded to the throne, the abbey was in all its glory; and on one occasion it furnished *two hundred* men, who went out under the command of one of the monks, named Friar Joly, to join the English armies and fight the Danes.

The English army was too small notwithstanding this desperate effort to strengthen it. They stood, however, all day in a compact band, protecting themselves with their shields from the arrows of the foot soldiers of the enemy, and with their pikes from the onset of the cavalry At night the Danes retired, as if giving up the

| A terrible battle. | Scene of consternation. |

contest; but as soon as the Saxons, now released from their positions of confinement and restraint, had separated a little, and began to fee. somewhat more secure, their implacable foes returned again and attacked them in separate masses, and with more fury than before. The Saxons endeavored in vain either to defend themselves or escape. As fast as their comrades were killed, the survivors stood upon the heaps of the slain, to gain what little advantage they could from so slight an elevation. Nearly all at length were killed. A few escaped into a neighboring wood, where they lay concealed during the day following, and then, when the darkness of the succeeding night came to enable them to conceal their journey, they made their way to the abbey, to make known to the anxious inmates of it the destruction of the army, and to warn them of the imminence of the impending danger to which they were now exposed.

A dreadful scene of consternation and terror ensued. The affrighted messengers told their tale, breathless and wayworn, at the door of the chapel, where the monks were engaged at their devotions. The aisles were filled with exclamations of alarm and despairing lamentations. The abbot, whose name was Theodore,

Proceedings at the monastery.   Part of the treasure sent away

immediately began to take measures suited to the emergency. He resolved to retain at the monastery only some aged monks and a few children, whose utter defenselessness, he thought, would disarm the ferocity and vengeance of the Danes. The rest, only about thirty, however, in number—nearly all the brethren having gone out under the Friar Joly into the great battle —were put on board a boat to be sent down the river. It seems at first view a strange idea to send away the vigorous and strong, and keep the infirm and helpless at the scene of danger; but the monks knew very well that all resistance was vain, and that, consequently, their greatest safety would lie in the absence of all appearance of the possibility of resistance.

The treasures were sent away, too, with all the men. They hastily collected all the valuables together, the relics, the jewels, and all of the gold and silver plate which could be easily removed, and placed them in a boat—packing them as securely as their haste and trepidation allowed. The boats glided down the river till they came to a lonely spot, where an anchorite or sort of hermit lived in solitude. The men and the treasures were to be intrusted to his charge. He concealed the men in the thickets

The remaining treasure concealed.   Abbot Theodore and the monks.

and other hiding-places in the woods, and buried the treasures.

In the mean time, as soon as the boats and the party of monks which accompanied them had left the abbey, the Abbot Theodore and the old monks that remained with him urged on the work of concealing that part of the treasures which had not been taken away. All of the plate which could not be easily transported, and a certain very rich and costly table employed for the service of the altar, and many sacred and expensive garments used by the higher priests in their ceremonies, had been left behind, as they could not be easily removed. These the abbot and the monks concealed in the most secure places that they could find, and then, clothing themselves in their priestly robes, they assembled in the chapel, and resumed their exercises of devotion. To be found in so sacred a place and engaged in so holy an avocation would have been a great protection from any Christian soldiery; but the monks entirely misconceived the nature of the impulses by which human nature is governed, in supposing that it would have any restraining influence upon the pagan Danes. The first thing the ferocious marauders did, on breaking into the sacred precincts of the chapel, was to cut down the venerable abbot at the altar, in his sacerdotal robes, and then to push forward the work of slaying every other inmate of the abbey, feeble and helpless as they were. Only one was saved.

This one was a boy, about ten years old. His name was Turgar. He was a handsome boy, and one of the Danish chieftains was struck with his countenance and air, in the midst of the slaughter, and took pity on him. The chieftain's name was Count Sidroc. Sidroc drew Turgar out of the immediate scene of danger, and gave him a Danish garment, directing him, at the same time, to throw aside his own, and then to follow him wherever he went, and keep close to his side, as if he were a Dane. The boy, relieved from his terrors by this hope of protection, obeyed implicitly. He followed Sidroc every where, and his life was saved. The Danes, after killing all the others, ransacked and plundered the monastery, broke open the tombs in their search for concealed treasures, and, after taking all that they could discover, they set the edifices on fire wherever they could find wood-work that would burn, and went away, leaving the bodies slowly burning in the grand and terrible funeral pile

From Crowland the marauders proceeded, taking Turgar with them, to another large and wealthy abbey in the neighborhood, which they plundered and destroyed, as they had the abbey at Crowland. Sidroc made Turgar his own attendant, keeping him always near him. When the expedition had completed their second conquest, they packed the valuables which they had obtained from both abbeys in wagons, and moved toward the south. It happened that some of these wagons were under Count Sidroc's charge, and were in the rear of the line of march. In passing a ford, the wheels of one of these rear wagons sank in the muddy bottom, and the horses, in attempting to draw the wagon out, became entangled and restive. While Sidroc's whole attention was engrossed by this difficulty, Turgar contrived to steal away unobserved. He hid himself in a neighboring wood, and, with a degree of sagacity and discretion remarkable in a boy of his years, he contrived to find his way back to the smoking ruins of his home at the Abbey of Crowland.

The monks who had gone away to seek concealment at the cell of the anchorite had returned, and were at work among the smoking ruins, saving what they could from the fire, and gathering together the blackened remains of their brethren for interment. They chose one of the monks that had escaped to succeed the abbot who had been murdered, repaired, so far as they could, their ruined edifices, and mournfully resumed their functions as a religious community.

Many of the tales which the ancient chroniclers tell of those times are romantic and incredible; they may have arisen, perhaps, in the first instance, in exaggerations of incidents and events which really occurred, and were then handed down from generation to generation by oral tradition, till they found historians to record them. The story of the martyrdom of King Edmund is of this character. Edmund was a sort of king over one of the nations of Anglo-Saxons called East Angles, who, as their name imports, occupied a part of the eastern portion of the island. Their particular hostility to Edmund was awakened, according to the story, in the following manner.

There was a certain bold and adventurous Dane named Lothbroc, who one day took his falcon on his arm and went out alone in a boat on the Baltic Sea, or in the straits connecting it with the German Ocean, intending to go to

LOTHBROC AND HIS FALCON.

a certain island and hunt. The falcon is a species of hawk which they were accustomed to train in those days, to attack and bring down birds from the air, and falconry was, as might have been expected, a very picturesque and exciting species of hunting. The game which Lothbroc was going to seek consisted of the wild fowl which frequents sometimes, in vast numbers, the cliffs and shores of the islands in those seas. Before he reached his hunting ground, however, he was overtaken by a storm, and his boat was driven by it out to sea. Accustomed to all sorts of adventures and dangers by sea and by land, and skilled in every operation required in all possible emergencies, Lothbroc contrived to keep his boat before the wind, and to bail out the water as fast as it came in, until at length, after being driven entirely across the German Ocean, he was thrown upon the English shore, where, with his hawk still upon his arm, he safely landed.

He knew that he was in the country of the most deadly foes of his nation and race, and accordingly sought to conceal rather than to make known his arrival. He was, however, found, after a few days, wandering up and down in a solitary wood, and was conducted, together with his hawk, to King Edmund.

Lothbroc taken into Edmund's service.   He is murdered by Beorn

Edmund was so much pleased with his air and bearing, and so astonished at the remarkable manner in which he had been brought to the English shore, that he gave him his life; and soon discovering his great knowledge and skill as a huntsman, he received him into his own service, and treated him with great distinction and honor. In addition to his hawk, Lothbroc had a greyhound, so that he could hunt with the king in the fields as well as through the air. The greyhound was very strongly attached to his master.

The king's chief huntsman at this time was Beorn, and Beorn soon became very envious and jealous of Lothbroc, on account of his superior power and skill, and of the honorable distinction which they procured for him. One day, when they two were hunting alone in the woods with their dogs, Beorn killed his rival, and hid his body in a thicket. Beorn went home, his own dogs following him, while the greyhound remained to watch mournfully over the body of his master. They asked Beorn what was become of Lothbroc, and he replied that he had gone off into the wood the day before, and he did not know what had become of him.

In the mean time, the greyhound remained

faithfully watching at the side of the body of his master until hunger compelled him to leave his post in search of food. He went home, and, as soon as his wants were supplied, he returned immediately to the wood again. This he did several days; and at length his singular conduct attracting attention, he was followed by some of the king's household, and the body of his murdered master was found.

The guilt of the murder was with little difficulty brought home to Beorn; and, as an appropriate punishment for his cruelty to an unfortunate and homeless stranger, the king condemned him to be put on board the same boat in which the ill-fated Lothbroc had made his perilous voyage, and pushed out to sea.

The winds and storms—entering, it seems, into the plan, and influenced by the same principles of poetical justice as had governed the king—drove the boat, with its terrified mariner, back again across to the mouth of the Baltic, as they had brought Lothbroc to England. The boat was thrown upon the beach, on Lothbroc's family domain.

Now Lothbroc had been, in his own country, a man of high rank and influence. He was of royal descent, and had many friends. He had two sons, men of enterprise and energy; and it so happened that the landing of Beorn took place so near to them, that the tidings soon came to their ears that their father's boat, in the hands of a Saxon stranger, had arrived on the coast. They immediately sought out the stranger, and demanded what had become of their father. Beorn, in order to hide his own guilt, fabricated a tale of Lothbroc's having been killed by Edmund, the king of the East Angles. The sons of the murdered Lothbroc were incensed at this news. They aroused their countrymen by calling upon them every where to aid them in revenging their father's death A large naval force was accordingly collected, and a formidable descent made upon the English coast.

Now Edmund, according to the story, was a humane and gentle-minded man, much more interested in deeds of benevolence and of piety than in warlike undertakings and exploits, and he was very far from being well prepared to meet this formidable foe. In fact, he sought refuge in a retired residence called Heglesdune. The Danes, having taken some Saxons captive in a city which they had sacked and destroyed, compelled them to make known the place of

State of England.

Edmund captured by the Danes. **His martyrdom**

the king's retreat. Hinquar, the captain of the Danes, sent him a summons to come and surrender both himself and all the treasures of his kingdom. Edmund refused. Hinquar then laid siege to the palace, and surrounded it; and, finally, his soldiers, breaking in, put Edmund's attendants to death, and brought Edmund himself, bound, into Hinquar's presence.

Hinquar decided that the unfortunate captive should die. He was, accordingly, first taken to a tree and scourged. Then he was shot at with arrows, until, as the account states, his body was so full of the arrows that remained in the flesh that there seemed to be no room for more During all this time Edmund continued to call upon the name of Christ, as if finding spiritual refuge and strength in the Redeemer in this his hour of extremity; and although these ejaculations afforded, doubtless, great support and comfort to him, they only served to irritate to a perfect phrensy of exasperation his implacable pagan foes. They continued to shoot arrows into him until he was dead, and then they cut off his head and went away, carrying the dissevered head with them. Their object was to prevent his friends from having the satisfaction of interring it with the body. They carried it to what they supposed a sufficient distance, and then threw it off into a wood by the way-side, where they supposed it could not easily be found.

As soon, however, as the Danes had left the place, the affrighted friends and followers of Edmund came out, by degrees, from their retreats and hiding places. They readily found the dead body of their sovereign, as it lay, of course, where the cruel deed of his murder had been performed. They sought with mournful and anxious steps, here and there, all around, for the head, until at length, when they came into the wood where it was lying, they heard, as the historian who records these events gravely testifies, a voice issuing from it, calling them, and directing their steps by the sound. They followed the voice, and, having recovered the head by means of this miraculous guidance, they buried it with the body.*

* A great many other tales are told of the miraculous phenomena exhibited by the body of St. Edmund, which well illustrate the superstitious credulity of those times. One writer says seriously that, when the head was found, a wolf had it, holding it carefully in his paws, with all the gentleness and care that the most faithful dog would manifest in guarding a trust committed to him by his master. This wolf followed the funeral procession to the tomb where the body was de-

| Credulity of mankind. | Commingling of piety and superstition. |

It seems surprising to us that reasonable men should so readily believe such tales as these; but there are, in all ages of the world, certain habits of belief, in conformity to which the whole community go together. We all believe whatever is in harmony with, or analogous to, the general type of faith prevailing in our own generation. Nobody could be persuaded now that a dead head could speak, or a wolf change his nature to protect it; but thousands will credit a fortune-teller, or believe that a mesmerized patient can have a mental perception of scenes and occurrences a thousand miles away.

There was a great deal of superstition in the days when Alfred was called to the throne, and there was also, with it, a great deal of genuine honest piety. The piety and the superstition, too, were inextricably intermingled and combined together. They were all Catholics then, yielding an implicit obedience to the Church of Rome, making regular contributions in money to sustain the papal authority, and looking to Rome as the great and central point of Christian influence and power, and the object of supreme

---

posited, and then disappeared. The head joined itself to the body again where it had been severed, leaving only a purple 'ine to mark the place of separation.

veneration. We have already seen that the Saxons had established a seminary at Rome, which King Ethelwolf, Alfred's father, rebuilt and re-endowed. One of the former Anglo-Saxon kings, too, had given a grant of one penny from every house in the kingdom to the successors of St. Peter at Rome, which tax, though nominally small, produced a very considerable sum in the aggregate, exceeding for many years the royal revenues of the kings of England. It continued to be paid down to the time of Henry VIII., when the reformation swept away that, and all the other national obligations of England to the Catholic Church together.

In the age of Alfred, however, there were not only these public acts of acknowledgment recognizing the papal supremacy, but there was a strong tide of personal and private feeling of veneration and attachment to the mother Church, of which it is hard for us, in the present divided state of Christendom, to conceive. The religious thoughts and affections of every pious heart throughout the realm centered in Rome. Rome, too, was the scene of many miracles, by which the imaginations of the superstitious and of the truly devout were ex-

Kenelm. — He is murdered by order of his sister

cited, which impressed them with an idea of power in which they felt a sort of confiding sense of protection. This power was continually interposing, now in one way and now in another, to protect virtue, to punish crime, and to testify to the impious and to the devout, to each in an appropriate way, that their respective deeds were the objects, according to their character, of the displeasure or of the approbation of Heaven.

On one occasion, the following incident is said to have occurred. The narration of it will illustrate the ideas of the time. A child of about seven years old, named Kenelm, succeeded to the throne in the Anglo-Saxon line. Being too young to act for himself, he was put under the charge of a sister, who was to act as regent until the boy became of age. The sister, ambitious of making the power thus delegated to her entirely her own, decided on destroying her brother. She commissioned a hired murderer to perpetrate the deed. The murderer took the child into a wood, killed him, and hid his body in a thicket, in a certain cow-pasture at a place called Clent. The sister then assumed the scepter in her own name, and suppressed all inquiries in respect to the fate of her brother; and his murder might have remained forever undiscovered, had it not been miraculously revealed at Rome.

A white dove flew into a church there one lay, and let fall upon the altar of St. Peter a paper, on which was written, in Anglo-Saxon characters,

𝔍𝔫 𝔈𝔩𝔢𝔫𝔱 𝔈𝔬𝔴-𝔟𝔞𝔱𝔠𝔥, 𝔅𝔢𝔫𝔢𝔩𝔪𝔢 𝔨𝔦𝔫𝔤 𝔟𝔢𝔞𝔯𝔫𝔢, 𝔩𝔦𝔢𝔱𝔥 𝔲𝔫𝔡𝔢𝔯 𝔈𝔥𝔬𝔯𝔫𝔢, 𝔥𝔢𝔞𝔡 𝔟𝔢𝔯𝔢𝔞𝔟𝔢𝔡.

For a time nobody could read the writing. At length an Anglo-Saxon saw it, and translated it into Latin, so that the pope and all others could understand it. The pope then sent a letter to the authorities in England, who made search and found the body.

But we must end these digressions, which we have indulged thus far in order to give the reader some distinct conception of the ideas and habits of the times, and proceed, in the next chapter, to relate the events immediately connected with Alfred's accession to the throne.

Chapter VI.

Alfred's Accession to the Throne

AT the battle in which Alfred's brother, Ethelred, whom Alfred succeeded on the throne, was killed, as is briefly mentioned at the close of chapter fourth, Alfred himself, then a brave and energetic young man, fought by his side. The party of Danes whom they were contending against in this fatal fight was the same one that came out in the expedition organized by the sons of Lothbroc, and whose exploits in destroying monasteries and convents were described in the last chapter. Soon after the events there narrated, this formidable body of marauders moved westward, toward that part of the kingdom where the dominions more particularly pertaining to the family of Alfred lay.

There was in those days a certain stronghold or castle on the River Thames, about forty miles west from London, which was not far from the confines of Ethelred's dominions. The large and populous town of Reading now stands upon the spot. It is at the confluence of the River

Thames with the Kennet, a small branch of the Thames, which here flows into it from the south. The spot, having the waters of the rivers for a defense upon two sides of it, was easily fortified. A castle had been built there, and, as usual in such cases, a town had sprung up about the walls.

The Danes advanced to this stronghold and took possession of it, and they made it for some time their head-quarters. It was at once the center from which they carried on their enterprises in all directions about the island, and the refuge to which they could always retreat when defeated and pursued. In the possession of such a fastness, they, of course, became more formidable than ever. King Ethelred determined to dislodge them. He raised, accordingly, as large a force as his kingdom would furnish, and, taking his brother Alfred as his second in command, he advanced toward Reading in a very resolute and determined manner.

He first encountered a large body of the Danes who were out on a marauding excursion. This party consisted only of a small detachment, the main body of the army of the Danes having been left at Reading to strengthen and complete the fortifications. They were digging a trench from

| The Danes fortify their castle. | They are defeated |

river to river, so as completely to insulate the castle, and make it entirely inaccessible on either side except by boats or a bridge. With the earth thrown out of the trench they were making an embankment on the inner side, so that an enemy, after crossing the ditch, would have a steep ascent to climb, defended too, as of course it would be in such an emergency, by long lines of desperate men upon the top, hurling at the assailants showers of javelins and arrows.

While, therefore, a considerable portion of the Danes were at work within and around their castle, to make it as nearly as possible impregnable as a place of defense, the detachment above referred to had gone forth for plunder, under the command of some of the bolder and more adventurous spirits in the horde. This party Ethelred overtook. A furious battle was fought. The Danes were defeated, and driven off the ground. They fled toward Reading. Ethelred and Alfred pursued them. The various parties of Danes that were outside of the fortifications, employed in completing the outworks, or encamped in the neighborhood, were surprised and slaughtered; or, at least, vast numbers of them were killed, and the rest retreated within the works—all maddened at their defeat, and burning with desire for revenge.

The Saxons were not strong enough to dispossess them of their fastness. On the contrary, in a few days, the Danes, having matured their plans, made a desperate sally against the Saxons, and, after a very determined and obstinate conflict, they gained the victory, and drove the Saxons off the ground. Some of the leading Saxon chieftains were killed, and the whole country was thrown into great alarm at the danger which was impending, that the Danes would soon gain the complete and undisputed possession of the whole land.

The Saxons, however, were not yet prepared to give up the struggle. They rallied their forces, gathered new recruits, reorganized their ranks, and made preparations for another struggle. The Danes, too, feeling fresh strength and energy in consequence of their successes, formed themselves in battle array, and, leaving their strong-hold, they marched out into the open country in pursuit of their foe. The two armies gradually approached each other and prepared for battle. Every thing portended a terrible conflict, which was to be, in fact, the great final struggle.

Æscesdune. —— The night before the battle

The place where the armies met was called in those times Æscesdune, which means Ashdown It was, in fact, a hill-side covered with ash trees. The name has become shortened and softened in the course of the ten centuries which have intervened since this celebrated battle, into Aston; if, indeed, as is generally supposed, the Aston of the present day is the locality of the ancient battle.

The armies came into the vicinity of each other toward the close of the day. They were both eager for the contest, or, at least, they pretended to be so, but they waited until the morning. The Danes divided their forces into two bodies. Two kings commanded one division, and certain chieftains, called *earls*, directed the other. King Ethelred undertook to meet this order of battle by a corresponding distribution of his own troops, and he gave, accordingly, to Alfred the command of one division, while he himself was to lead the other. All things being thus arranged, the hum and bustle of the two great encampments subsided at last, at a late hour, as the men sought repose under their rude tents, in preparation for the fatigues and exposures of the coming day. Some slept; others watched restlessly, and talked together, sleepless under the influence of that strange excitement, half exhilaration and half fear, which prevails in a camp on the eve of a battle. The camp fires burned brightly all the night, and the sentinels kept vigilant watch, expecting every moment some sudden alarm.

The night passed quietly away. Ethelred and Alfred both arose early. Alfred went out to arouse and muster the men in his division of the encampment, and to prepare for battle. Ethelred, on the other hand, sent for his priest, and, assembling the officers in immediate attendance upon him, commenced divine service in his tent—the service of the mass, according to the forms and usages which, even in that early day, were prescribed by the Catholic Church. Alfred was thus bent on immediate and energetic action, while Ethelred thought that the hour for putting forth the exertion of human strength did not come until time had been allowed for completing, in the most deliberate and solemn manner, the work of imploring the protection of Heaven.

Ethelred seems by his conduct on this occasion to have inherited from his father, even more than Alfred, the spirit of religious devotion at least so far as the strict and faithful observance of religious forms was concerned There was, it is true, a particular reason in this case why the forms of divine service should be faithfully observed, and that is, that the war was considered in a great measure a religious war. The Danes were pagans. The Saxons were Christians. In making their attacks upon the dominions of Ethelred, the ruthless invaders were animated by a special hatred of the name of Christ, and they evinced a special hostility toward every edifice, or institution, or observance which bore the Christian name. The Saxons, therefore, in resisting them, felt that they were not only fighting for their own possessions and for their own lives, but that they were defending the kingdom of God, and that he, looking down from his throne in the heavens, regarded them as the champions of his cause; and, consequently, that he would either protect them in the struggle, or, if they fell, that he would receive them to mansions of special glory and happiness in heaven, as martyrs who had shed their blood in his service and for his glory.

Taking this view of the subject, Ethelred, instead of going out to battle at the early dawn, collected his officers into his tent, and formed them into a religious congregation. Alfred, on

Alfred's impetuosity.   *His great ability*

the other hand, full of impetuosity and ardor, was arousing his men, animating them by his words of encouragement and by the influence of his example, and making, as energetically as possible, all the preparations necessary for the approaching conflict.

In fact, Alfred, though his brother was king, and he himself only a lieutenant general under him, had been accustomed to take the lead in all the military operations of the army, on account of the superior energy, resolution, and tact which he evinced, even in this early period of his life. His brothers, though they retained the scepter, as it fell successively into their hands, relied mainly on his wisdom and courage in all their efforts to defend it, and Ethelred may have been somewhat more at his ease, in listening to the priest's prayers in his tent, from knowing that the arrangements for marshaling and directing a large part of the force were in such good hands.

The two encampments of Alfred and Ethelred seem to have been at some little distance from each other. Alfred was impatient at Ethelred's delay. He asked the reason for it. They told him that Ethelred was attending mass, and that he had said he should on no ac-

Battle of Æscesdune.　　　　　　　*Flight of the Danes*

count leave his tent until the service was concluded. Alfred, in the mean time, took possession of a gentle elevation of land, which now would give him an advantage in the conflict. A single thorn-tree, growing there alone, marked the spot. The Danes advanced to attack him, expecting that, as he was not sustained by Ethelred's division of the army, he would be easily overpowered and driven from his post.

Alfred himself felt an extreme and feverish anxiety at Ethelred's delay. He fought, however, with the greatest determination and bravery. The thorn-tree continued to be the center of the conflict for a long time, and, as the morning advanced, it became more and more doubtful how it would end. At last, Ethelred, having finished his devotional services, came forth from his camp at the head of his division, and advanced vigorously to his faltering brother's aid. This soon decided the contest. The Danes were overpowered and put to flight. They fled at first in all directions, wherever each separate band saw the readiest prospect of escape from the immediate vengeance of their pursuers. They soon, however, all began with one accord to seek the roads which would conduct them to their stronghold at Reading. They were madly

Results of the battle.   *Alfred and Ethelred*

pursued, and massacred as they fled, by Alfred's and Ethelred's army. Vast numbers fell. The remnant secured their retreat, shut themselves up within their walls, and began to devote their eager and earnest attention to the work of repairing and making good their defenses.

This victory changed for the time being the whole face of affairs, and led, in various ways, to very important consequences, the most important of which was, as we shall presently see, that it was the means indirectly of bringing Alfred soon to the throne. As to the cause of the victory, or, rather, the manner in which it was accomplished, the writers of the times give very different accounts, according as their respective characters incline them to commend, in man, a feeling of quiet trust and confidence in God when placed in circumstances of difficulty or danger, or a vigorous and resolute exertion of his own powers. Alfred looked for deliverance to the determined assaults and heavy blows which he could bring to bear upon his pagan enemies with weapons of steel around the thorntree in the field. Ethelred trusted to his hope of obtaining, by his prayers in his tent, the effectual protection of Heaven; and they who have written the story differ, as they who read it will,

The old chronicles.   *The locality of the battle.*

on the question to whose instrumentality the victory is to be ascribed. One says that Alfred gained it by his sword. Another, that Alfred exerted his strength and his valor in vain, and was saved from defeat and destruction only by the intervention of Ethelred, bringing with him the blessing of Heaven.

In fact, the various narratives of these ancient events, which are found at the present day in the old chronicles that record them, differ always very essentially, not only in respect to matters of opinion, and to the point of view in which they are to be regarded, but also in respect to questions of fact. Even the place where this battle was fought, notwithstanding what we have said about the derivation of Aston from Æscesdune, is not absolutely certain. There is in the same vicinity another town, called Ashbury, which claims the honor. One reason for supposing that this last is the true locality is that there are the ruins of an ancient monument here, which, tradition says, was a monument built to commemorate the death of a Danish chieftain slain here by Alfred. There is also in the neighborhood another very singular monument, called The White Horse, which also nas the reputation of having been fashioned to commemorate Alfred's victories. The White Horse is a rude representation of a horse, formed by cutting away the turf from the steep slope of a hill, so as to expose a portion of the white surface of the chalky rock below of such a form that the figure is called a horse, though they who see it seem to think it might as well have been called a dog. The name, however, of *The White Horse* has come down with it from ancient times, and the hill on which it is cut is known as The White Horse Hill. Some ingenious antiquarians think they find evidence that this gigantic profile was made to commemorate the victory obtained by Alfred and Ethelred over the Danes at the ancient Æscesdune.

However this may be, and whatever view we may take of the comparative influence of Alfred's energetic action and Ethelred's religious faith in the defeat of the Danes at this great battle, it is certain that the results of it were very momentous to all concerned. Ethelred received a wound, either in this battle or in some of the smaller contests and collisions which followed it, under the effects of which he pined and lingered for some months, and then died. Alfred, by his decision and courage on the day of the battle, and by the ardor and rea-

Alfred's popularity. | *He is selected to succeed Ethelred*

olution with which he pressed all the subsequent operations during the period of Ethelred's decline, made himself still more conspicuous in the eyes of his countrymen than he had ever been before. In looking forward to Ethelred's approaching death, the people, accordingly, began to turn their eyes to Alfred as his successor. There were children of some of his older brothers living at that time, and they, according to all received principles of hereditary right, would naturally succeed to the throne; but the nation seems to have thought that the crisis was too serious, and the dangers which threatened their country were too imminent, to justify putting any child upon the throne. The accession of one of those children would have been the signal for a terrible and protracted struggle among powerful relatives and friends for the regency during the minority of the youthful sovereign, and this, while the Danes remained in their strong-hold at Reading, in daily expectation of new re-enforcements from beyond the sea, would have plunged the country in hopeless ruin. They turned their eyes toward Alfred, therefore, as the sovereign to whom they were to bow so soon as Ethelred should cease to breathe.

The Danes strengthen themselves. *Their successes*

In the mean time, the Danes, far from being subdued by the adverse turn of fortune which had befallen them, strengthened themselves in their fortress, made desperate sallies from their intrenchments, attacked their foes on every possible occasion, and kept the country in continual alarm. They at length so far recruited their strength, and intimidated and discouraged their foes, whose king and nominal leader, Ethelred, was now less able than ever to resist them, as to take the field again. They fought more pitched battles; and, though the Saxon chroniclers who narrate these events are very reluctant to admit that the Saxons were really vanquished in these struggles, they allow that the Danes kept the ground which they successively took post upon, and the discouraged and disheartened inhabitants of the country were forced to retire.

In the mean time, too, new parties of Danes were continually arriving on the coast, and spreading themselves in marauding and plundering excursions over the country. The Danes at Reading were re-enforced by these bands, which made the conflict between them and Ethelred's forces more unequal still. Alfred did his utmost to resist the tide of ill fortune, with the limited and doubtful authority which he

Death of Ethelred. *His burial at Wimborne*

held; but all was in vain. Ethelred, worn down, probably, with the anxiety and depression which the situation of his kingdom brought upon him, lingered for a time, and then died, and Alfred was by general consent called to the throne. This was in the year 871.

It was a matter of moment to find a safe and secure place of deposit for the body of Ethelred, who, as a Christian slain in contending with pagans, was to be considered a martyr. His memory was honored as that of one who had sacrificed his life in defense of the Christian faith. They knew very well that even his lifeless remains would not be safe from the vengeance of his foes unless they were placed effectually beyond the reach of these desperate marauders. There was, far to the south, in Dorsetshire, on the southern coast of England, a monastery, at Wimborne, a very sacred spot worthy to be selected as a place of royal sepulture. The spot has continued sacred to the present day; and it has now upon the site, as is supposed, of the ancient monastery, a grand cathedral church or minster, full of monuments of former days, and impressing all beholders with its solemn architectural grandeur. Here they conveyed the body of Ethelred and inter red it. It was a place of sacred seclusion, where there reigned a solemn stillness and awe, which no *Christian* hostility would ever have dared to disturb. The sacrilegious paganism of the Danes, however, would have respected it but little, if they had ever found access to it; out they did not. The body of Ethelred remained undisturbed; and, many centuries afterward, some travelers who visited the spot recorded the fact that there was a monument there with this inscription:

"IN HOC LOCO QUIESC'T CORPUS ETHELREDI REGIS WEST SAXONUM, MARTYRIS, QUI ANNO DOMINI DCCCLXXI., XXIII. APRILIS, PER MANUS DANORUM PAGANORUM, OCCUBUIT."*

Such is the commonly received opinion of the death of Ethelred. And yet some of the critical historians of modern times, who find cause to doubt or disbelieve a very large portion of what is stated in ancient records, attempt to prove that Ethelred was not killed by the Danes at all, but that he died of the plague, which terrible disease was at that time prevailing in that part of England. At all events, he died, and Alfred, his brother, was called to reign in his stead.

* "Here rests the body of Ethelred, king of West Saxony the Martyr, who died by the hands of the pagan Danes, in the year of our Lord 871."

Chapter VII.

Reverses.

THE historians say that Alfred was very unwilling to assume the crown when the death of Ethelred presented it to him. If it had been an object of ambition or desire, there would probably have been a rival claimant, whose right would perhaps have proved superior to his own, since it appears that one or more of the brothers who reigned before him left a son, whose claim to the inheritance, if the inheritance had been worth claiming, would have been stronger than that of their uncle. The *son* of the oldest son takes precedence always of the *brother*, for hereditary rights, like water, never move laterally so long as they can continue to descend.

The nobles, however, and chieftains, and all the leading powers of the kingdom of Wessex, which was the particular kingdom which descended from Alfred's ancestors, united to urge Alfred to take the throne. His father had, indeed, designated him as the successor of his brothers by his will, though how far a monarch may properly control by his will the disposal of his realm, is a matter of great uncertainty Alfred yielded at length to these solicitations, and determined on assuming the sovereign power. He first went to Wimborne to attend to the funeral solemnities which were to be observed at his royal brother's burial. He then went to Winchester, which, as well as Wimborne, is in the south of England, to be crowned and anointed king. Winchester was, even in those early days, a great ecclesiastical center. It was for some time the capital of the West Saxon realm. It was a very sacred place, and the crown was there placed upon Alfred's head, with the most imposing and solemn ceremonies. It is a curious and remarkable fact, that the spots which were consecrated in those early days by the religious establishments of the times, have preserved in almost every case their sacredness to the present day. Winchester is now famed all over England for its great Cathedral church, and the vast religious establishment which has its seat there—the annual revenues and expenditures of which far exceed those of many of the states of this Union. The income of the bishop alone was for many years double

CORONATION CHAIR.

that of the salary of the President of the United States. The Bishop of Winchester is widely celebrated, therefore, all over England, for his wealth his ecclesiastical power, the architectural grandeur of the Cathedral church, and the wealth and importance of the college of ecclesiastics over which he presides.

It was in Winchester that Alfred was crowned. As soon as the ceremony was performed, he took the field, collected his forces, and went to meet the Danes again. He found the country in a most deplorable condition. The Danes had extended and strengthened their positions. They had got possession of many of the towns, and, not content with plundering castles and abbeys, they had seized lands, and were beginning to settle upon them, as if they intended to make Alfred's new kingdom their permanent abode. The forces of the Saxons, on the other hand, were scattered and discouraged. There seemed no hope left to them of making head against their pestiferous invaders. If they were defeated, their cruel conquerors showed no moderation and no mercy in their victory; and if they conquered, it was only to suppress for a moment one horde, with a certainty of being attacked immediately by another, more recently arrived, and more determined and relentless than those before them.

Alfred succeeded, however, by means of the influence of his personal character, and by the very active and efficient exertions that he made, in concentrating what forces remained, and in preparing for a renewal of the contest. The first great battle that was fought was at Wilton. This was within a month of his accession to the throne. The battle was very obstinately fought; at the first onset Alfred's troops carried all before them, and there was every prospect that he would win the day. In the end, however, the tide of victory turned in favor of the Danes, and Alfred and his troops were driven from the field. There was an immense loss on both sides. In fact, both armies were, for the time, pretty effectually disabled, and each seems to have shrunk from a renewal of the contest Instead, therefore, of fighting again, the two commanders entered into negotiations. Hubba was the name of the Danish chieftain. In the end, he made a treaty with Alfred, by which he agreed to retire from Alfred's dominions, and leave him in peace, provided that Alfred would not interfere with him in his wars in any other part of England. Alfred's kingdom was Wessex Besides Wessex, there was Essex, Mercia, and Northumberland. Hubba and his Danes, finding that Alfred was likely to prove too formidable an antagonist for them easily to subdue, thought it would be most prudent to give up one kingdom out of the four, on condition of not having Alfred to contend against in their depredations upon the other three. They accordingly made the treaty, and the Danes withdrew. They evacuated their posts and strong-holds in Wessex, and went down the Thames to London, which was in Mercia, and there commenced a new course of conquest and plunder, where they had no such powerful foe to oppose them.

Buthred was the king of Mercia. He could not resist Hubba and his Danes alone, and he could not now have Alfred's assistance. Alfred was censured very much at the time, and has been condemned often since, for having thus made a separate peace for himself and his own immediate dominions, and abandoned his natural allies and friends, the people of the other Saxon kingdoms. To make a peace with savage and relentless pagans, on the express condition of leaving his fellow-Christian neighbors at their mercy, has been considered ungenerous, at least, if it was not unjust. On the other

Buthred's misfortunes. — *He buys off the Danes*

hand, those who vindicate his conduct maintain that it was his duty to secure the peace and welfare of his own realm, leaving other sovereigns to take care of theirs; and that he would have done very wrong to sacrifice the property and lives of his own immediate subjects to a mere point of honor, when it was utterly out of his power to protect them and his neighbors too.

However this may be, Buthred, finding that he could not have Alfred's aid, and that he could not protect his kingdom by any force which he could himself bring into the field, tried negotiations too, and he succeeded in buying off the Danes with money. He paid them a large sum, on condition of their leaving his dominions finally and forever, and not coming to molest him any more. Such a measure as this is always a very desperate and hopeless one. Buying off robbers, or beggars, or false accusers, or oppressors of any kind, is only to encourage them to come again, after a brief interval, under some frivolous pretext, with fresh demands or new oppressions, that they may be bought off again with higher pay. At least Buthred found it so in this case. Hubba went northward for a time, into the kingdom of Northumberland, and, after various conquests and

Buthred's unhappy end. *Ceolwulf*

plunderings there, he came back again into Mercia, on the plea that there was a scarcity of provisions in the northern kingdom, and he was *obliged* to come back. Buthred bought him off again with a larger sum of money. Hubba scarcely left the kingdom this time, but spent the money with his army, in carousings and excesses, and then went to robbing and plundering as before. Buthred, at last, reduced to despair, and seeing no hope of escape from the terrible pest with which his kingdom was infested, abandoned the country and escaped to Rome. They received him as an exiled monarch, in the Saxon school, where he soon after died a prey to grief and despair.

The Danes overturned what remained of Buthred's government. They destroyed a famous mausoleum, the ancient burial place of the Mercian kings. This devastation of the abodes of the dead was a sort of recreation—a savage amusement, to vary the more serious and dangerous excitements attending their contests with the living. They found an officer of Buthred's government named Ceolwulf, who, though a Saxon, was willing, through his love of place and power, to accept of the office of king in subordination to the Danes, and hold it at their disposal, paying an annual tribute to them. Ceolwulf was execrated by his countrymen, who considered him a traitor. He, in his turn, oppressed and tyrannized over them.

In the mean time, a new leader, with a fresh horde of Danes, had landed in England. His name was Halfden. Halfden came with a considerable fleet of ships, and, after landing his men, and performing various exploits and encountering various adventures in other parts of England, he began to turn his thoughts toward Alfred's dominions. Alfred did not pay particular attention to Halfden's movements at first, as he supposed that his treaty with Hubba had bound the whole nation of the Danes not to encroach upon *his* realm, whatever they might do in respect to the other Saxon kingdoms. Alfred had a famous castle at Wareham, on the southern coast of the island. It was situated on a bay which lies in what is now Dorsetshire. This castle was the strongest place in his dominions. It was garrisoned and guarded, but not with any special vigilance, as no one expected an attack upon it. Halfden brought his fleet to the southern shore of the island, and, organizing an expedition there, he put to sea, and before any one suspected his de-

Wareham Castle taken by Halfden.   *Contests and truces*

sign, he entered the bay, surprised and attacked Wareham Castle, and took it. Alfred and the people of his realm were not only astonished and alarmed at the loss of the castle, but they were filled with indignation at the treachery of the Danes in violating their treaty by attacking it. Halfden said, however, that he was an independent chieftain, acting in his own name, and was not bound at all by any obligations entered into by Hubba!

There followed after this a series of contests and truces, during which treacherous wars alternated with still more treacherous and illusive periods of peace, neither party, on the whole, gaining any decided victory. The Danes, at one time, after agreeing upon a cessation of hostilities, suddenly fell upon a large squadron of Alfred's horse, who, relying on the truce, were moving across the country too much off their guard. The Danes dismounted and drove off the men, and seized the horses, and thus provided themselves with cavalry, a species of force which it is obvious they could not easily bring, in any ships which they could then construct, across the German Ocean. Without waiting for Alfred to recover from the surprise and consternation which this unexpected treach-

The town of Exeter. — *It is taken by the Danes*

ery occasioned, the newly-mounted troop of Danes rode rapidly along the southern coast of England till they came to the town of Exeter Its name was in those days Exancester. It was then, as it is now, a very important town. It has since acquired a mournful celebrity as the place of refuge, and the scene of suffering of Queen Henrietta Maria, the mother of Charles the Second.* The loss of this place was a new and heavy cloud over Alfred's prospects It placed the whole southern coast of his realm in the hands of his enemies, and seemed to portend for the whole interior of the country a period of hopeless and irremediable calamity.

It seems, too, from various unequivocal statements and allusions contained in the narratives of the times, that Alfred did not possess, during this period of his reign, the respect and affection of his subjects. He is accused, or, rather, not directly accused, but spoken of as generally known to be guilty of many faults which alien ated the hearts of his countrymen from him, and prepared them to consider his calamities as the judgments of Heaven. He was young and ardent, full of youthful impetuosity and fire, and

---

* For an account of Henrietta's adventures and sufferings at Exeter, see the History of Charles II., chap. iii

was elated at his elevation to the throne; and, during the period while the Danes left him in peace, under the treaties he had made with Hubba, he gave himself up to pleasure, and not always to innocent pleasure. They charged him, too, with being tyrannical and oppressive in his government, being so devoted to gratifying his own ambition and love of personal indulgence that he neglected his government, sacrificed the interests and the welfare of his subjects, and exercised his regal powers in a very despotic and arbitrary manner.

It is very difficult to decide, at this late day how far this disposition to find fault with Alfred's early administration of his government arose from, or was aggravated by, the misfortunes and calamities which befell him. On the one hand, it would not be surprising if, young, and arduous, and impetuous as he was at this period of his life, he should have fallen into the errors and faults which youthful monarchs are very prone to commit on being suddenly raised to power. But then, on the other hand, men are prone, in all ages of the world, and most especially in such rude and uncultivated times as these were, to judge military and governmental action by the sole criterion of success.

Saint Neot. — He reproaches Alfred with his misdeeds

Thus, when they found that Alfred's measures, one after another, failed in protecting his country, that the impending calamities burst successively upon them, notwithstanding all Alfred's efforts to avert them, it was natural that they should look at and exaggerate his faults, and charge all their national misfortunes to the influence of them.

There was a certain Saint Neot, a kinsman and religious counselor of Alfred, the history of whose life was afterward written by the Abbot of Crowland, the monastery whose destruction by the Danes was described in a former chapter. In this narrative it is said that Neot often rebuked Alfred in the severest terms for his sinful course of life, predicting the most fatal consequences if he did not reform, and using language which only a very culpable degree of remissness and irregularity could justify. "You glory," said he, one day, when addressing the king, "in your pride and power, and are determined and obdurate in your iniquity. But there is a terrible retribution in store for you I entreat you to listen to my counsels, amend your life, and govern your people with moderation and justice, instead of tyranny and oppression, and thus avert if you can, before it is too late, the impending judgments of Heaven."

Justice of Neot's reproaches.   *Alfred's early sins atoned for.*

Such language as this it is obvious that only a very serious dereliction of duty on Alfred's part could call for or justify; but, whatever he may have done to deserve it, his offenses were so fully expiated by his subsequent sufferings, and he atoned for them so nobly, too, by the wisdom, the prudence, the faithful and devoted patriotism of his later career, that mankind have been disposed to pass by the faults of his early years without attempting to scrutinize them too closely. The noblest human spirits are always, in some periods of their existence, or in some aspects of their characters, strangely weakened by infirmities and frailties, and deformed by sin. This is human nature. We like to imagine that we find exceptions, and to see specimens of moral perfection in our friends or in the historical characters whose general course of action we admire; but there are no exceptions. To err and to sin, at some times and in some ways, is the common, universal, and inevitable lot of humanity.

At the time when Halfden and his followers seized Wareham Castle and Exeter, Alfred had been several years upon the throne, during which time these derelictions from duty took place, so far as they existed at all. But now.

Alfred arouses himself. Convenes an assembly of chiefs and nobles

alarmed at the imminence of the impending danger, which threatened not only the welfare of his people, but his own kingdom and even his life—for one Saxon monarch had been driven from his dominions, as we have seen, and had died a miserable exile at Rome—Alfred aroused himself in earnest to the work of regaining his lost influence among his people, and recovering their alienated affections.

He accordingly, as his first step, convened a great assembly of the leading chieftains and noblemen of the realm, and made addresses to them, in which he urged upon them the imminence of the danger which threatened their common country, and pressed them to unite vigorously and energetically with him to contend against their common foe. They must make great sacrifices, he said, both of their comfort and ease, as well as of their wealth, to resist successfully so imminent a danger. He summoned them to arms, and urged them to contribute the means necessary to pay the expense of a vigorous prosecution of the war. These harangues, and the ardor and determination which Alfred manifested himself at the time of making them, were successful. The nation aroused itself to new exertions, and for a time

THE FIRST BRITISH FLEET.

Alfred builds a fleet. Difficulty of procuring seamen.

there was a prospect that the country would be saved.

Among the other measures to which Alfred resorted in this emergency was the attempt to encounter the Danes upon their own element by building and equipping a fleet of ships, with which to proceed to sea, in order to meet and attack upon the water certain new bodies of invaders, who were on the way to join the Danes already on the island—coming, as rumor said, along the southern shore. In attempting to build up a naval power, the greatest difficulty, always, is to provide seamen. It is much easier to build ships than to train sailors. To man his little fleet, Alfred had to enlist such half-savage foreigners as could be found in the ports, and even pirates, as was said, whom he induced to enter his service, promising them pay, and such plunder as they could take from the enemy. These attempts of Alfred to build and man a fleet are considered the first rude beginnings from which the present vast edifice of British naval power took its origin. When the fleet was ready to put to sea, the people thronged the shores, watching its movements with the utmost curiosity and interest, earnestly hoping that it might be successful in its contests with the more tried and experienced armaments with which it would have to contend.

Alfred was, in fact, successful in the first enterprises which he undertook with his ships. He encountered a fleet of the Danish ships in the Channel, and defeated them. His fleet captured, moreover, one of the largest of the vessels of the enemy; and, with what would be thought in our day unpardonable cruelty, they threw the sailors and soldiers whom they found on board into the sea, and kept the vessel.

After all, however, Alfred gained no conclusive and decisive victory over his foes. They were too numerous, too scattered, and too firmly seated in the various districts of the island, of some of which they had been in possession for many years. Time passed on, battles were fought, treaties of peace were made, oaths were taken, hostages were exchanged, and then, after a very brief interval of repose, hostilities would break out again, each party bitterly accusing the other of treachery. Then the poor hostages would be slain, first by one party, and after ward, in retaliation, by the other.

In one of these temporary and illusive pacifications, Alfred attempted to bind the Danes by Christian oaths. Their customary mode of

binding themselves, in cases where they wished
to impose a solemn religious obligation, was to
swear by a certain ornament which they wore
upon their arms, which is called in the chronicles of those times a *bracelet*. What its form
and fashion was we can not now precisely know;
but it is plain that they attached some superstitious, and perhaps idolatrous associations of
sacredness to it. To swear by this bracelet was
to place themselves under the most solemn obligation that they could assume. Alfred, however, not satisfied with this pagan sanction,
made them, in confirming one treaty, swear by
the Christian relics, which were certain supposed memorials of our Saviour's crucifixion, or
portions of the bodies of dead saints miraculously preserved, and to which the credulous
Christians of that day attached an idea of sacredness and awe, scarcely less superstitious
than that which their pagan enemies felt for
the bracelets on their arms. Alfred could not
have supposed that these treacherous covenant-
ers, since they would readily violate the faith
plighted in the name of what they revered,
could be held by what they hated and despised.
Perhaps he thought that, though they would be
no more likely to keep the new oath than the

old, still, that their violation of it, when it occurred, would be in itself a great crime—that his cause would be subsequently strengthened by their thus incurring the special and unmitigated displeasure of Heaven.

Among the Danish chieftains with whom Alfred had thus continually to contend in this early part of his reign, there was one very famous hero, whose name was Rollo. He invaded England with a wild horde which attended him for a short time, but he soon retired and went to France, where he afterward greatly distinguished himself by his prowess and his exploits. The Saxon historians say that he retreated from England because Alfred gave him such a reception that he saw that it would be impossible for him to maintain his footing there. His account of it was, that, one day, when he was perplexed with doubt and uncertainty about his plans, he fell asleep and dreamed that he saw a swarm of bees flying southward. This was an omen, as he regarded it, indicating the course which he ought to pursue. He accordingly embarked his men on board his ships again, and crossed the Channel, and sought successfully in Normandy, a province of France the kingdom and the home which, either on account of Alfred or of the bees, he was not to enjoy in England.

The cases, however, in which the Danish chieftains were either entirely conquered or finally expelled from the kingdom were very few. As years passed on, Alfred found his army diminishing, and the strength of his kingdom wasting away. His resources were exhausted, his friends had disappeared, his towns and castles were taken, and, at last, about eight years after his coronation at Winchester as monarch of the most powerful of the Saxon kingdoms, he found himself reduced to the very last extreme of destitution and distress.

Chapter VIII.
The Seclusion.

NOTWITHSTANDING the tide of disaster and calamity which seemed to be gradually overwhelming Alfred's kingdom, he was not reduced to absolute despair, but continued for a long time the almost hopeless struggle. There is a certain desperation to which men are often aroused in the last extremity, which surpasses courage, and is even sometimes a very effectual substitute for strength; and Alfred might, perhaps, have succeeded, after all, in saving his affairs from utter ruin, had not a new circumstance intervened, which seemed at once to extinguish all remaining hope and to seal his doom.

This circumstance was the arrival of a new band of Danes, who were, it seems, more numerous, more ferocious, and more insatiable than any who had come before them. The other kingdoms of the Saxons had been already pretty effectually plundered. Alfred's kingdom of Wessex was now, therefore, the most inviting field, and, after various excursions of co

Alfred's army disorganized.   *He is left alone.*

quest and plunder in other parts of the island, they came like an inundation over Alfred's frontiers, and all hope of resisting them seems to have been immediately abandoned. The Saxon armies were broken up. Alfred had lost, it appears, all influence and control over both leaders and men. The chieftains and nobles fled. Some left the country altogether; others hid themselves in the best retreats and fastnesses that they could find. Alfred himself was obliged to follow the general example. A few attendants, either more faithful than the rest. or else more distrustful of their own resources and inclined, accordingly, to seek their own personal safety by adhering closely to their sovereign, followed him. These, however, one after another, gradually forsook him, and, finally, the fallen and deserted monarch was left alone.

In fact, it was a relief to him at last to be left alone; for they who remained around him became in the end a burden instead of affording him protection. They were too few to fight, and too many to be easily concealed. Alfred withdrew himself from them, thinking that, under the circumstances in which he was now placed, he was justified in seeking his own personal safety alone. He had a wife, whom he

Alfred's wife. *He retires to Athelney*

married when he was about twenty years old; but she was not with him now, though she afterward joined him. She was in some other place of retreat. She could, in fact, be much more easily concealed than her husband; for the Danes, though they would undoubtedly have valued her very highly as a captive, would not search for her with the eager and persevering vigilance with which it was to be expected they would hunt for their most formidable, but now discomfited and fugitive foe.

Alfred, therefore, after disentangling himself from all but one or two trustworthy and faithful friends, wandered on toward the west, through forests, and solitudes, and wilds, to get as far away as possible from the enemies who were upon his track. He arrived at last on the remote western frontiers of his kingdom, at a place whose name has been immortalized by its having been for some time the place of his retreat. It was called Athelney.* Athelney was, however, scarcely deserving of a name, for it was nothing but a small spot of dry land in the midst of a morass, which, as grass would

---

* The name is spelled variously, Ethelney, Æthelney Ethelingay, &c. It was in Somersetshire, between the rivers Thone and Parrot.

The cow-herd.   He gives Alfred an asylum.

grow upon it in the openings among the trees, a simple cow-herd had taken possession of, and built his hut there.

The solid land which the cow-herd called his farm was only about two acres in extent. All around it was a black morass, of great extent, wooded with alders, among which green sedges grew, and sluggish streams meandered, and mossy tracts of verdure spread treacherously over deep bogs and sloughs. In the driest season of the summer the goats and the sheep penetrated into these recesses, but, excepting in the devious and tortuous path by which the cow-herd found his way to his island, it was almost impassable for man.

Alfred, however, attracted now by the impediments and obstacles which would have repelled a wanderer under any other circumstances, went on with the greater alacrity the more intricate and entangled the thickets of the morass were found, since these difficulties promised to impede or deter pursuit. He found his way in to the cow-herd's hut. He asked for shelter People who live in solitudes are always hospitable. The cow-herd took the wayworn fugitive in, and gave him food and shelter. Alfred remained his guest for a considerable time

The story is, that after a few days the cow-herd asked him who he was, and how he came to be wandering about in that distressed and destitute condition. Alfred told him that he was one of the king's *thanes.* A thane was a sort of chieftain in the Saxon state. He accounted for his condition by saying that Alfred's army had been beaten by the Danes, and that he, with the other generals, had been forced to fly. He begged the cow-herd to conceal him, and to keep the secret of his character until times should change, so that he could take the field again.

The story of Alfred's seclusion on the *island,* as it might almost be called, of Ethelney, is told very differently by the different narrators of it. Some of these narrations are inconsistent and contradictory. They all combine, however, though they differ in respect to many other incidents and details, in relating the far-famed story of Alfred's leaving the cakes to burn. It seems that, though the cow-herd himself was allowed to regard Alfred as a man of rank in disguise—though even *he* did not know that it was the king—his wife was not admitted, even in this partial way, into the secret. She was made to consider the stranger as some common strolling

Alfred's occupations at Ethelney. *His gloomy thoughts.*

countryman, and the better to sustain this idea, he was taken into the cow-herd's service, and employed in various ways, from time to time, in labors about the house and farm. Alfred's thoughts, however, were little interested in these occupations. His mind dwelt incessantly upon his misfortunes and the calamities which had befallen his kingdom. He was harassed by continual suspense and anxiety, not being able to gain any clear or certain intelligence about the condition and movements of either his friends or foes. He was revolving continually vague and half-formed plans for resuming the command of his army and attempting to regain his kingdom, and wearying himself with fruitless attempts to devise means to accomplish these ends. Whenever he engaged voluntarily in any occupation, it would always be something in harmony with these trains of thought and these plans. He would repair and put in order implements of hunting, or any thing else which might be deemed to have some relation to war. He would make bows and arrows in the chimney corner—lost, all the time, in melancholy reveries, or in wild and visionary schemes of future exploits.

One evening, while he was thus at work, the

cow-herd's wife left, for a few moments, some cakes under his charge, which she was baking upon the great stone hearth, in preparation for their common supper. Alfred, as might have been expected, let the cakes burn. The woman, when she came back and found them smoking, was very angry. She told him that he could eat the cakes fast enough when they were baked, though it seemed he was too lazy and good for nothing to do the least thing in helping to bake them. What wide-spread and lasting effects result sometimes from the most trifling and inadequate causes! The singularity of such an adventure befalling a monarch in disguise, and the terse antithesis of the reproaches with which the woman rebuked him, invest this incident with an interest which carries it every where spontaneously among mankind. Millions, within the last thousand years, have heard the name of Alfred, who have known no more of him than this story; and millions more, who never would have heard of him but for this story, have been led by it to study the whole history of his life; so that the unconscious cowherd's wife, in scolding the disguised monarch for forgetting her cakes, was perhaps doing

ALFRED WATCHING THE CAKES.

Various accounts of the story of the cakes.

more than he ever did himself for the wide extension of his future fame.*

* As this incident has been so famous, it may amuse the reader to peruse the different accounts which are given of it in the most ancient records which now remain. They were written in Latin and in Saxon, and, of course, as given here, they are translations. The discrepancies which the reader will observe in the details illustrate well the uncertainty which pertains to all historical accounts that go back to so early an age.

"He led an unquiet life there, at his cow-herd's. It happened that, on a certain day, the rustic wife of the man prepared to bake her bread. The king, sitting then near the hearth, was making ready his bow and arrows, and other warlike implements, when the ill-tempered woman beheld the loaves burning at the fire. She ran hastily and removed them, scolding at the king, and exclaiming, 'You man! you will not turn the bread you see burning, but you will be very glad to eat it when it is done!' This unlucky woman little thought she was addressing the King Alfred."

In a certain Saxon history the story is told thus:

'He took shelter in a swain's house, and also him and his evil wife diligently served. It happened that, on one day, the swain's wife heated her oven, and the king sat by it warming himself by the fire. She knew not then that he was the king. Then the evil woman was excited, and spoke to the king with an angry mind. 'Turn thou these loaves, that they burn not, for I see daily that thou art a great eater!' He soon obeyed this evil woman because she would scold. He then the good king, with great anxiety and sighing, called to his Lord, imploring his pity."

The following account is from a Latin life of St. Neot which still exists in manuscript, and is of great antiquity.

Various accounts of the story of the cakes.

Alfred was, for a time, extremely depressed and disheartened by the sense of his misfortunes

"Alfred, a fugitive, and exiled from his people, came by chance and entered the house of a poor herdsman, and there remained some days concealed, poor and unknown.

"It happened that, on the Sabbath day, the herdsman, as usual, led his cattle to their accustomed pastures, and the king remained alone in the cottage with the man's wife. She, as necessity required, placed a few loaves, which some call *loudas*, on a pan, with fire underneath, to be baked for her husband's repast and her own, on his return.

"While she was necessarily busied, like peasants, on other offices, she went anxious to the fire, and found the bread burning on the other side. She immediately assailed the king with reproaches. 'Why, man! do you sit thinking there, and are too proud to turn the bread? Whatever be your family, with your manners and sloth, what trust can be put in you hereafter? If you were even a nobleman, you will be glad .o eat the bread which you neglect to attend to.' The king, though stung by her upbraidings, yet heard her with patience and mildness, and, roused by her scolding, took care to bake her bread thereafter as she wished."

There is one remaining account, which is as follows:

"It happened that the herdsman one day, as usual, led his swine to their accustomed pasture, and the king remained at home alone with the wife. She placed her bread under the ashes of the fire to bake, and was employed in other business when she saw the loaves burning, and said to the king in her rage, 'You will not turn the bread you see burning, though you will be very glad to eat it when done!' The king, with a submitting countenance, though vexed at her upbraidings not only turned the bread, but gave them to the woman well baked and unbroken."

It is obvious, from the character of these several accounts

Effect of Alfred's seclusion on his heart and character.

and calamities; but the monkish writers who described his character and his life say that the influence of his sufferings was extremely salutary in softening his disposition and improving his character. He had been proud, and haughty, and domineering before. He became humble, docile, and considerate now. Faults of character that are superficial, resulting from the force of circumstances and peculiarities of temptation, rather than from innate depravity of heart, are easily and readily burned off in the fire of affliction, while the same severe ordeal seems only to indurate the more hopelessly those propensities which lie deeply seated in an inherent and radical perversity.

---

that each writer, taking the substantial fact as the groundwork of his story, has added such details and chosen such expressions for the housewife's reproaches as suited his own individual fancy. We find, unfortunately for the truth and trustworthiness of history, that this is almost always the case, when independent and original accounts of past transactions, whether great or small, are compared. The gravest historians, as well as the lightest story tellers, frame their narrations for *effect*, and the tendency in all ages to shape and fashion the narrative with a view to the particular effect designed by the individual narrator to be produced has been found entirely irresistible. It is necessary to compare, with great diligence and careful scrutiny, a great many different accounts, in order to learn how little there is to be exactly and confidently believed.

| Alfred's patience and fortitude. | He makes himself known. |

Alfred, though restless and wretched in his apparently hopeless seclusion, bore his privations with a great degree of patience and fortitude, planning, all the time, the best means of reorganizing his scattered forces, and of rescuing his country from the ruin into which it had fallen. Some of his former friends, roaming as he himself had done, as fugitives about the country, happened at length to come into the neighborhood of his retreat. He heard of them, and cautiously made himself known. They were rejoiced to find their old commander once more, and, as there was no force of the Danes in that neighborhood at the time, they lingered, timidly and fearlessly at first, in the vicinity, until, at length, growing more bold as they found themselves unmolested in their retreat, they began to make it their gathering place and head-quarters. Alfred threw off his disguise, and assumed his true character Tidings of his having been thus discovered spread confidentially among the most tried and faithful of his Saxon followers, who had themselves been seeking safety in other places of refuge. They began, at first cautiously and by stealth, but afterward more openly, to repair to the spot Alfred's family, too, from which he had now

Scarcity of provisions.   *Services of the herdsman.*

been for many months entirely separated, contrived to rejoin him. The herdsman, who proved to be a man of intelligence and character superior to his station, entered heartily into all these movements. He kept the secret faithfully. He did all in his power to provide for the wants and to promote the comfort of his warlike guests, and, by his fidelity and devotion, laid Alfred under obligations of gratitude to him, which the king, when he was afterward restored to the throne, did not forget to repay.

Notwithstanding, however, all the efforts which the herdsman made to obtain supplies, the company now assembled at Ethelney were sometimes reduced to great straits. There were not only the wants of Alfred and his immediate family and attendants to be provided for, but many persons were continually coming and going, arriving often at unexpected times, and acting, as roving and disorganized bodies of soldiers are very apt to do at such times, in a very inconsiderate manner. The herdsman's farm produced very little food, and the inaccessibleness of its situation made it difficult to bring in supplies from without. In fact, it was necessary, in one part of the approach to it, to use a boat, so that the place is generally called, in history, an island, though it was insulated mainly by swamps and morasses rather than by navigable waters. There were, however, sluggish streams all around it, where Alfred's men, when their stores were exhausted, went to fish, under the herdsman's guidance, returning sometimes with a moderate fare, and sometimes with none.

The monks who describe this portion of Alfred's life have recorded an incident as having occurred on the occasion of one of these fishing excursions, which, however, is certainly, in part, a fabrication, and may be wholly so. It was in the winter. The waters about the grounds were frozen up. The provisions in the house were nearly exhausted, there being scarcely any thing remaining. The men went away with their fishing apparatus, and with their bows and arrows, in hopes of procuring some fish or fowl to replenish their stores. Alfred was left alone, with only a single lady of his family, who is called in the account "Mother," though it could not have been Alfred's own mother, as she had been dead many years. Alfred was sitting in the hut reading. A beggar, who had by some means or other found his way in over the frozen morasses, came to the door, and asked for food. Alfred, looking up from his book, asked the

Alfred's charity.   *His dream.*

mother, whoever she was, to go and see what there was to give him. She went to make examination, and presently returned, saying that there was nothing to give him. There was only a single loaf of bread remaining, and that would not be half enough for their own wants that very night when the hunting party should return, if they should come back unsuccessful from their expedition. Alfred hesitated a moment, and then ordered half the loaf to be given to the beggar. He said, in justification of the act, that his trust was now in God, and that the power which once, with five loaves and two small fishes, fed abundantly three thousand men, could easily make half a loaf suffice for them.

The loaf was accordingly divided, the beggar was supplied, and, delighted with this unexpected relief, he went away. Alfred turned his attention again to his reading. After a time the book dropped from his hand. He had fallen asleep. He dreamed that a certain saint appeared to him, and made a revelation to him from heaven. God, he said, had heard his prayers, was satisfied with his penitence, and pitied his sorrows; and that his act of charity in relieving the poor beggar, even at the risk of

Return of the hunting party.   *Revival of Alfred's hopes.*

leaving himself and his friends in utter destitution, was extremely acceptable in the sight of Heaven. The faith and trust which he thus manifested were about to be rewarded. The time for a change had come. He was to be restored to his kingdom, and raised to a new and higher state of prosperity and power than before. As a token that this prediction was true, and would be all fulfilled, the hunting party would return that night with an ample and abundant supply.

Alfred awoke from his sleep with his mind filled with new hopes and anticipations. The hunting party returned loaded with supplies. and in a state of the greatest exhilaration at their success. They had fish and game enough to have supplied a little army. The incident of relieving the beggar, the dream, and their unwonted success confirming it, inspired them all with confidence and hope. They began to form plans for commencing offensive operations. They would build fortifications to strengthen their position on the island. They would collect a force. They would make sallies to attack the smaller parties of the Danes. They would send agents and emissaries about the kingdom to arouse, and encourage, and assem-

Plans of Alfred and his friends to recover the kingdom.

ble such Saxon forces as were yet to be found. In a word, they would commence a series of measures for recovering the country from the possession of its pestilent enemy, and for restoring the rightful sovereign to the throne. The development of these projects and plans, and the measures for carrying them into effect, were very much hastened by an event which suddenly occurred in the neighborhood of Ethelney, the account of which, however, must be postponed to the next chapter.

Chapter IX.

Reassembling of the Army.

ETHELNEY, though its precise locality can not now be certainly ascertained, was in the southwestern part of England, in Somersetshire, which county lies on the southern shore of the Bristol Channel. There is a region of marshes in that vicinity, which tradition assigns as the place of Alfred's retreat; and there was, about the middle of this century, a farmhouse there, which bore the name of Ethelney, though this name may have been given to it in modern times by those who imagined it to be the ancient locality. A jewel of gold, engraved as an amulet to be worn about the neck, and inscribed with the Saxon words which mean "Alfred had me made," was found in the vicinity, and is still carefully preserved in a museum in England. Some curious antiquarians profess to find the very hillock, rising out of the low grounds around, where the herdsman that entertained Alfred so long lived; but this, of course is all uncertain. The peculiarities of

Changes produced by time.   *Alfred fortifies Ethelney.*

the spot derived their character from the morasses and the woods, and the courses of the sluggish streams in the neighborhood, and these are elements of landscape scenery which ten centuries of time and of cultivation would entirely change.

Whatever may have been the precise situation of the spot, instead of being, as at first, a mere hiding-place and retreat, it became, before many months, as was intimated in the last chapter, a military camp, secluded and concealed, it is true, but still possessing, in a considerable degree, the characteristics of a fastness and place of defense. Alfred's company erected something which might be called a wall. They built a bridge across the water where the herdsman's boat had been accustomed to ply. They raised two towers to watch and guard the bridge. All these defenses were indeed of a very rude and simple construction; still, they answered the purpose intended. They afforded a real protection; and, more than all, they produced a certain moral effect upon the minds of those whom they shielded, by enabling them to consider themselves as no longer lurking fugitives, dependent for safety on simple concealment, but as a garrison, weak, it is true, but still gathering strength, and advancing gradually toward a condition which would enable them to make positive aggressions upon the enemy.

The circumstance which occurred to hasten the development of Alfred's plans, and which was briefly alluded to at the close of the last chapter, was the following: It seems that quite a large party of Danes, under the command of a leader named Hubba, had been making a tour of conquest and plunder in Wales, which country was on the other side of the Bristol Channel, directly north of Ethelney, where Alfred was beginning to concentrate a force. He would be immediately exposed to an attack from this quarter as soon as it should be known that he was at Ethelney, as the distance across the Channel was not great, and the Danes were provided with shipping.

Ethelney was in the county called Somersetshire. To the southwest of Somersetshire, a little below it, on the shores of the Bristol Channel, was a castle, called Castle Kenwith, in Devonshire. The Duke of Devonshire, who held this castle, encouraged by Alfred's preparations for action, had assembled a considerable force here, to be ready to co-operate with Al-

Hubba crosses the Channel.   *He besieges Odun.*

fred in the active measures which he was about to adopt. Things being in this state, Hubba brought down his forces to the northern shores of the Channel, collected together all the boats and shipping that he could command, crossed the Channel, and landed on the Devonshire shore. Odun, the duke, not being strong enough to resist, fled, and shut himself up, with all his men, in the castle. Hubba advanced to the castle walls, and, sitting down before them, began to consider what to do.

Hubba was the last surviving son of Ragner Lodbrog, whose deeds and adventures were related in a former chapter. He was, like all other chieftains among the Danes, a man of great determination and energy, and he had made himself very celebrated all over the land by his exploits and conquests. His particular horde of marauders, too, was specially celebrated among all the others, on account of a mysterious and magical banner which they bore. The name of this banner was the *Reafan*, that is, the Raven. There was the figure of a raven woven or embroidered on the banner. Hubba's three sisters had woven it for their brothers, when they went forth across the German Ocean to avenge their father's death. It possessed, a

| The magical banner. | How regarded by the Saxons and Danes |

both the Danes and Saxons believed, supernatural and magical powers. The raven on the banner could foresee the result of any battle into which it was borne. It remained lifeless and at rest whenever the result was to be adverse; and, on the other hand, it fluttered its wings with a mysterious and magical vitality when they who bore it were destined to victory. The Danes consequently looked up to this banner with a feeling of profound veneration and awe, and the Saxons feared and dreaded its mysterious power. The explanation of this pretended miracle is easy. The imagination of superstitious men, in such a state of society as that of these half-savage Danes, is capable of much greater triumphs over the reason and the senses than is implied in making them believe that the wings of a bird are either in motion or at rest, whichever it fancies, when the banner on which the image is embroidered is advancing to the field and fluttering in the breeze.

The Castle of Kenwith was situated on a rocky promontory, and was defended by a Saxon wall. Hubba saw that it would be difficult to carry it by a direct assault. On the other hand it was not well supplied with water or provisions, and the numerous multitude which had

Hubba's plan of operations. — *Preparations of Odun*

crowded into it, would, as Hubba thought, be speedily compelled to surrender by thirst and famine, if he were simply to wait a short time, till their scanty stock of food was consumed. Perhaps the raven did not flutter her wings when Hubba approached the castle, but by her apparent lifelessness portended calamity if an attack were to be made. At all events, Hubba decided not to attack the castle, but to invest it closely on all sides, with his army on the land and with his vessels on the side of the sea, and thus reduce it by famine. He accordingly stationed his troops and his galleys at their posts and established himself in his tent, quietly to await the result.

He did not have to wait so long as he anticipated. Odun, finding that his danger was so imminent, nay, that his destruction was inevitable if he remained in his castle, thus shut in, determined, in the desperation to which the emergency reduced him, to make a sally. Accordingly, one night, as soon as it was dark, so that the indications of any movement within the castle might not be perceived by the sentinels and watchmen in Hubba's lines, he began to marshal and organize his army for a sudden and furious onset upon the camp of the Danes.

They waited, when all was ready, till the first break of day. To make the surprise most effectual, it was necessary that it should take place in the night; but then, on the other hand, the success, if they should be successful, would require, in order to be followed up with advantage, the light of day. Odun chose, therefore, the earliest dawn as the time for his attempt, as this was the only period which would give him at first darkness for his surprise, and afterward light for his victory. The time was well chosen, the arrangements were all well made, and the result corresponded with the character of the preparations. The sally was triumphantly successful.

The Danes, who were all, except their sentinels, sleeping quietly and secure, were suddenly aroused by the unearthly and terrific yells with which the Saxons burst into the lines of their encampment. They flew to arms, but the shock of the onset produced a panic and confusion which soon made their cause hopeless. Odun and his immediate followers pressed directly forward into Hubba's tent, where they surprised the commander, and massacred him on the spot. They seized, too, to their inexpressible joy, the sacred banner, which was in

Capture of the banner.   Slaughter of the Danes.

Hubba's tent, and bore it forth, rejoicing in it, not merely as a splendid trophy of their victory, but as a loss to their enemies which fixed and sealed their doom.

The Danes fled before their enemies in terror, and the consternation which they felt, when they learned that their banner had been captured and their leader slain, was soon changed into absolute despair. The Saxons slew them without mercy, cutting down some as they were running before them in their headlong flight, and transfixing others with their spears and arrows as they lay upon the ground, trampled down by the crowds and the confusion. There was no place of refuge to which they could fly except to their ships. Those, therefore, that escaped the weapons of their pursuers, fled in the direction of the water, where the strong and the fortunate gained the boats and the galleys, while the exhausted and the wounded were drowned. The fleet sailed away from the coast, and the Saxons, on surveying the scene of the terrible contest, estimated that there were twelve hundred dead bodies lying in the field.

This victory, and especially the capture of the Raven, produced vast effects on the minds both of the Saxons and of the Danes, animat-

| Alfred's prospects brightening. | Alarm of the Danes |

ing and encouraging the one, and depressing the other with superstitious as well as natural and proper fears. The influence of the battle was sufficient, in fact, wholly to change Alfred's position and prospects. The news of the discovery of the place of his retreat, and of the measures which he was maturing for taking the field again to meet his enemies, spread throughout the country. The people were every where ready to take up arms and join him. There were large bodies of Danes in several parts of his dominions still, and they, alarmed somewhat at these indications of new efforts of resistance on the part of their enemies, began to concentrate their strength and prepare for another struggle.

The main body of the Danes were encamped at a place called Edendune, in Wiltshire. There is a hill near, which the army made their main position, and the marks of their fortifications have been traced there, either in imagination or reality, in modern times. Alfred wished to gain more precise and accurate information than he yet possessed of the numbers and situation of his foes; and, in order to do this, instead of employing a spy, he conceived the design of going himself in disguise to explore his

Alfred resolves to explore the Danish camp.	His disguise

camp of the Danes. The undertaking was full of danger, but yet not quite so desperate as at first it might seem. Alfred had had abundant opportunities during the months of his seclusion to become familiar with the modes of speech and the manners of peasant life. He had also, in his early years, stored his memory with Saxon poetry, as has already been stated. He was fond of music, too, and well skilled in it; so that he had every qualification for assuming the character of one of those roving harpers, who, in those days, followed armies, to sing songs and make amusement for the soldiers. He determined, consequently, to assume the disguise of a harper, and to wander into the camp of the Danes, that he might make his own observations on the nature and magnitude of the force with which he was about to contend.

He accordingly clothed himself in the garb of the character which he was to assume, and, taking his harp upon his shoulder, wandered away in the direction of the Northmen's camp. Such a strolling countryman, half musician, half beggar would enter without suspicion or hinderance into the camp, even though he belonged to the nation of the enemy. Alfred was readily admitted, and he wandered at will about the lines, to play and sing to the soldiers wherever he found groups to listen—intent, apparently, on nothing but his scanty pittance of pay, while he was really studying, with the utmost attention and care, the number, and disposition, and discipline of the troops, and all the arrangements of the army. He came very near discovering himself, however, by overacting his part. His music was so well executed and his ballads were so fine, that reports of the excellence of his performance reached the commander's ears. He ordered the pretended harper to be sent into his tent, that he might hear him play and sing. Alfred went, and thus he had the opportunity of completing his observations in the tent, and in the presence of the Danish king.

Alfred found that the Danish camp was in a very unguarded and careless condition. The name of the commander, or king, was Guthrum.* Alfred, while playing in his presence, studied his character, and it is improbable that the very extraordinary course which he afterward pursued in respect to Guthrum may have been caused, in a great degree, by the opportu-

* Spelled sometimes Godrun, Gutrum, Gythram, and in various other ways.

Guthrum's reception of Alfred. His attendant and companion.

nity he now enjoyed of domestic access to him and of obtaining a near and intimate view of his social and personal character. Guthrum treated the supposed harper with great kindness. He was much pleased both with his singing and his songs, being attracted, too, probably, in some degree, by a certain mysterious interest which the humble stranger must have inspired; for Alfred possessed personal and intellectual traits of character which could not but have given to his conversation and his manners a certain charm, notwithstanding all his efforts to disguise or conceal them.

However this may be, Guthrum gave Alfred a very friendly reception, and the hour of social intercourse and enjoyment which the general and the ballad-singer spent together was only a precursor of the more solid and honest friendship which afterward subsisted between them as allied sovereigns.

Alfred had one person with him, whom he had brought from Ethelney—a sort of attendant—to help him carry his harp, and to be a companion for him on the way. He would have needed such a companion even if he had been only what he seemed; but for a spy, going in disguise into the camp of such ferocious enemies as the Danes, it would seem absolutely indispensable that he should have the support and sympathy of a friend.

Alfred, after finishing his examination of the camp of Guthrum, and forming secretly, in his own mind, his plans for attacking it, moved leisurely away, taking his harp and his attendant with him, as if going on in search of some new place to practice his profession. As soon as he was out of the reach of observation, he made a circuit and returned in safety to Ethelney. The season was now spring, and every thing favored the commencement of his enterprise.

His first measure was to send out some trusty messengers into all the neighboring counties, to visit and confer with his friends at their various castles and strong-holds. These messengers were to announce to such Saxon leaders as they should find that Alfred was still alive, and that he was preparing to take the field against the Danes again; and were to invite them to assemble at a certain place appointed, in a forest, with as many followers as they could bring, that the king might there complete the organization of an army, and hold consultation with them to mature their plans

| Selwood Forest. | Stone of Egbert. |

The wood on the borders of which they were to meet was an extensive forest of willows, fifteen miles long and six broad It was known by the name of Selwood Forest. There was a celebrated place called the Stone of Egbert, where the meeting was to be held. Each chieftain whom the messengers should visit was to be invited to come to the Stone of Egbert at the appointed day, with as many armed men, and yet in as secret and noiseless a manner as possible, so as thus, while concentrating all their forces in preparation for their intended attack, to avoid every thing which would tend to put Guthrum on his guard.

The messengers found the Saxon chieftains very ready to enter into Alfred's plans. They were rejoiced to hear, as some of them did now for the first time hear, that he was alive, and that the spirit and energy of his former character were about to be exhibited again. Every thing, in fact, conspired to favor the enterprise. The long and gloomy months of winter were past, and the opening spring brought with it, as usual, excitement and readiness for action. The tidings of Odun's victory over Hubba, and the capture of the sacred raven, which had spread every where, had awakened a general enthusiasm, and a desire on the part of all the Saxon chieftains and soldiers to try their strength once more with their ancient enemies.

Accordingly, those to whom the secret was intrusted eagerly accepted the invitation, or, perhaps, as it should rather be expressed, obeyed the summons which Alfred sent them. They marshaled their forces without any delay, and repaired to the appointed place in Selwood Forest. Alfred was ready to meet them there. Two days were occupied with the arrivals of the different parties, and in the mutual congratulations and rejoicings. Growing more bold as their sense of strength increased with their increasing numbers, and with the ardor and enthusiasm which their mutual influence on each other inspired, they spent the intervals of their consultations in festivities and rejoicings, celebrating the occasion with games and martial music. The forest resounded with the blasts of horns, the sound of the trumpets, the clash of arms, and the shouts of joy and congratulation, which all the efforts of the more prudent and cautious could not repress.

In the mean time, Guthrum remained in his encampment at Edendune. This seems to have been the principal concentration of the forces

Guthrum in his camp. *His sense of security*

of the Danes which were marshaled for military service; and yet there were large numbers of the people, disbanded soldiers, or non-combatants, who had come over in the train of the armies, that had taken possession of the lands which they had conquered, and had settled upon them for cultivation, as if to make them their permanent home. These intruders were scattered in larger or smaller bodies in various parts of the kingdom, the Saxon inhabitants being prevented from driving them away by the influence and power of the armies, which still kept possession of the field, and preserved their military organization complete, ready for action at any time whenever any organized Saxon force should appear.

Guthrum, as we have said, headed the largest of these armies. He was aware of the increasing excitement that was spreading among the Saxon population, and he even heard rumors of the movements which the bodies of Saxons made, in going under their several chieftains to Selwood Forest. He expected that some important movement was about to occur, but he had no idea that preparations so extended, and for so decisive a demonstration, were so far advanced. He remained, therefore, at

Alfred marches toward Guthrum's camp. — **He encamps at Æcglea.**

his camp at Edendune, gradually completing his arrangements for his summer campaign, but making no preparations for resisting any sudden or violent attack.

When all was ready, Alfred put himself at the head of the forces which had collected at the Egbert Stone, or, as it is quaintly spelled in some of the old accounts, Ecgbyrth-stan. There is a place called Brixstan in that vicinity now, which may possibly be the same name modified and abridged by the lapse of time. Alfred moved forward toward Guthrum's camp He went only a part of the way the first day intending to finish the march by getting into the immediate vicinity of the enemy on the morrow. He succeeded in accomplishing this object, and encamped the next night at a place called Æcglea,* on an eminence from which he could reconnoiter, from a great distance, the position of the army.

That night, as he was sleeping in his tent, he had a remarkable dream. He dreamed that his relative, St. Neot, who has been already mentioned as the chaplain or priest who reprov-

---

* Some think that this place is the modern Leigh; others, that it was Highley; either of which names might have been deduced from Æcglea

ed him so severely for his sins in the early part of his reign, appeared to him. The apparition bid him not fear the immense army of pagans whom he was going to encounter on the morrow. God, he said, had accepted his penitence, and was now about to take him under his special protection. The calamities which had befallen him were sent in judgment to punish the pride and arrogance which he had manifested in the early part of his reign; but his faults had been expiated by the sufferings he had endured, and by the penitence and the piety which they had been the means of awakening in his heart; and now he might go forward into the battle without fear, as God was about to give him the victory over all his enemies.

The king related his dream the next morning to his army. The enthusiasm and ardor which the chieftains and the men had felt before were very much increased by this assurance of success. They broke up their encampment, therefore, and commenced the march, which was to bring them, before many hours, into the presence of the enemy, with great alacrity and eager expectations of success.

Chapter X.

The Victory over the Danes.

ENCOURAGED by his dream, and animated by the number and the elation of his followers, Alfred led his army onward toward the part of the country where the camp of the enemy lay. He intended to surprise them; and, although Guthrum had heard vague rumors that some great Saxon movement was in train, he viewed the sudden appearance of this large and well-organized army with amazement.

He had possession of the hill near Edendune, which has been already described. He had established his head-quarters here, and made his strongest fortifications on the summit of the eminence. The main body of his forces, were, however, encamped upon the plain, over which they extended, in vast numbers, far and wide. Alfred halted his men to change the order of march into the order of battle. Here he made an address to his men. As no time was to be lost, he spoke but a few words. He reminded

| The battle. | Defeat of the Danes |

them that they were to contend, that day, to rescue themselves and their country from the intolerable oppression of a horde of pagan idolaters ; that God was on their side, and had promised them the victory ; and he urged them to act like men, so as to deserve the success and happiness which was in store for them.

The army then advanced to the attack, the Danes having been drawn out hastily, but with as much order as the suddenness of the call would allow, to meet them. When near enough for their arrows to take effect, the long line of Alfred's troops discharged their arrows. They then advanced to the attack with lances ; but soon these and all other weapons which kept the combatants at a distance were thrown aside, and it became a terrible conflict with swords, man to man.

It was not long before the Danes began to yield. They were not sustained by the strong assurance of victory, nor by the desperate determination which animated the Saxons. The flight soon became general. They could not gain the fortification on the hill, for Alfred had forced his way in between the encampment on the plains and the approaches to the hill. The Danes, consequently, not being able to find ref uge in either part of the position they had taken, fled altogether from the field, pursued by Alfred's victorious columns as fast as they could follow.

Guthrum succeeded, by great and vigorous exertions, in rallying his men, or, at least, in so far collecting and concentrating the separate bodies of the fugitives as to change the flight into a retreat, having some semblance of military order. Vast numbers had been left dead upon the field. Others had been taken prisoners. Others still had become hopelessly dispersed, having fled from the field of battle in diverse directions, and wandered so far, in their terror, that they had not been able to rejoin their leader in his retreat. Then, great numbers of those who pressed on under Guthrum's command, exhausted by fatigue, or spent and fainting from their wounds, sank down by the way-side to die, while their comrades, intent only upon their own safety, pressed incessantly on. The retreating army was thus, in a short time, reduced to a small fraction of its original force. This remaining body, with Guthrum at their head, continued their retreat until they reached a castle which promised them protection. They poured in over the drawbridges

The Danes shut themselves up in a castle.	Elation of the Saxons

and through the gates of this fortress in extreme confusion; and feeling suddenly, and for the moment, entirely relieved at their escape from the imminence of the immediate danger, they shut themselves in.

The finding of such a retreat would .ave been great good fortune for these wretched fugitives if there had been any large force in the country to come soon to their deliverance; but, as they were without provisions and without water, they soon began to perceive that, unless they obtained some speedy help from without, they had only escaped the Saxon lances and swords to die a ten times more bitter death of thirst and famine; and there was no force to relieve them. The army which had been thus defeated was the great central force of the Danes upon the island. The other detachments and independent bands which were scattered about the land were thunderstruck at the news of this terrible defeat. The Saxons, too, were every where aroused to the highest pitch of enthusiasm at the reappearance of their king and the tidings of his victory. The whole country was in arms. Guthrum, however, shut up in his castle, and closely invested with Alfred's forces, had no means of knowing what was

24—13

Hopeless condition of the Danes.   **Surrender of Guthrum.**

passing without. His numbers were so small in comparison with those besieging him that it would have been madness for him to have attempted a sally; and he would not surrender. He waited day after day, hoping against hope that some succor would come. His half-famished sentinels gazed from the watch-towers of the castle all around, looking for some cloud of distant dust, or weapon glancing in the sun, which might denote the approach of friends coming to their rescue. This lasted fourteen days. At the end of that time, the number within this wretched prison who were raving in the delirium of famine and thirst, or dying in agony, became too great for Guthrum to persist any longer. He surrendered. Alfred was once more in possession of his kingdom.

During the fourteen days that elapsed between the victory on the field of battle and the final surrender of Guthrum, Alfred, feeling that the power was now in his hands, had had ample time to reflect on the course which he should pursue with his subjugated enemies; and the result to which he came, and the measure which he adopted, evince, as much as any act of his life, the greatness, and originality, and nobleness of his character. Here were two distinct

Saxon Victory.

The Saxons and Danes equally aggressors. Their relations

and independent races on the same island, that had been engaged for many years in a most fierce and sanguinary struggle, each gaining at times a temporary and partial victory, but neither able entirely to subdue or exterminate the other. The Danes, it is true, might be considered as the aggressors in this contest, and, as such, wholly in the wrong; but then, on the other hand, it was to be remembered that the ancestors of the Saxons had been guilty of precisely the same aggressions upon the Britons, who held the island before them; so that the Danes were, after all, only intruding upon intruders. It was, besides, the general maxim of the age, that the territories of the world were prizes open for competition, and that the right to possess and to govern vested naturally and justly in those who could show themselves the strongest. Then, moreover, the Danes had been now for many years in Britain. Vast numbers had quietly settled on agricultural lands. They had become peaceful inhabitants. They had established, in many cases, friendly relations with the Saxons. They had intermarried with them; and the two races, instead of appearing, as at first, simply as two hostile armies of combatants contending on the field, had been, for some years, acquiring the character of a mixed population, established and settled, though heterogeneous, and, in some sense, antagonistic still To root out all these people, intruders though they were, and send them back again across the German Ocean, to regions where they no longer had friends or home, would have been a desperate—in fact, an impossible undertaking.

Alfred saw all these things. He took, in fact, a general, and comprehensive, and impartial view of the whole subject, instead of regarding it, as most conquerors in his situation would have done, in a *partisan*, that is, an exclusively *Saxon* point of view He saw how impossible it was to undo what had been done, and wisely determined to take things as they were, and make the best of the present situation of affairs, leaving the past, and aiming only at accomplishing the best that was now attainable for the future. It would be well if all men who are engaged in quarrels which they vainly endeavor to settle by discussing and disputing about what is past and gone, and can now never be recalled, would follow his example. In all such cases we should say, let the past be forgotten, and, taking things as they now are, .er

Alfred's generosity.   Terms offered Guthrum

us see what we can do to secure peace and happiness in future.

The policy which Alfred determined to adopt was, not to attempt the utter extirpation of the Danes from England, but only to expel the *armed forces* from his own dominions, allowing those peaceably disposed to remain in quiet possession of such lands in other parts of the island as they already occupied. Instead, therefore, of treating Guthrum with harshness and severity as a captive enemy, he told him that he was willing not only to give him his liberty, out to regard him, on certain conditions, as a friend and an ally, and allow him to reign as a king over that part of England which his countrymen possessed, and which was beyond Alfred's own frontiers. These conditions were, that Guthrum was to go away with all his forces and followers out of Alfred's kingdom, under solemn oaths never to return; that he was to confine himself thenceforth to the southeastern part of England, a territory from which the Saxon government had long disappeared; that he was to give hostages for the faithful fulfillment of these stipulations, without, however receiving on his part any hostages from Alfred. There was one other stipulation, more **extraor-**

Guthrum agrees to become a Christian.   Sudden change in his affairs

dinary than all the rest, viz., that Guthrum should become a convert to Christianity, and publicly avow his adhesion to the Saxon faith by being baptized in the presence of the leaders of both armies, in the most open and solemn manner. In this proposed baptism, Alfred himself would stand his godfather.

This idea of winning over a pagan soldier to the Christian Church as the price of his ransom from famine and death in the castle to which his direst enemy had driven him—this enemy himself, the instrument thus of so rude a mode of conversion, to be the sponsor of the new communicant's religious profession — was one in keeping, it is true, with the spirit of the times, but still it is one which, under the circumstances of this case, only a mind of great originality and power would have conceived of or attempted to carry into effect. Guthrum might well be astonished at this unexpected turn in his affairs. A few days before, he saw himself on the brink of utter and absolute destruction Shut up with his famished soldiers in a gloomy castle, with the enemy, bitter and implacable, as he supposed, thundering at the gates, the only alternatives before him seemed to be to die of starvation and phrensy within the walls which covered him, or by a cruel military execution in the event of surrender. He surrendered at last, as it would seem, only because the utmost that human cruelty can inflict is more tolerable than the horrid agonies of thirst and hunger.

We can not but hope that Alfred was led, in some degree, by a generous principle of Christian forgiveness in proposing the terms which he did to his fallen enemy, and also that Guthrum, in accepting them, was influenced, in part at least, by emotions of gratitude and by admiration of the high example of Christian virtue which Alfred thus exhibited. At any rate, he did accept them. The army of the Danes were liberated from their confinement, and commenced their march to the eastward; Guthrum himself, attended by thirty of his chiefs and many other followers, became Alfred's guest for some weeks, until the most pressing measures for the organization of Alfred's government could be attended to, and the necessary preparations for the baptism could be made. At length, some weeks after the surrender, the parties all repaired together, now firm friends and allies, to a place near Ethelney, where the ceremony of baptism was to be performed.

The admission of this pagan chieftain into the Christian Church did not probably mark any real change in his opinions on the question of paganism and Christianity, but it was not the less important in its consequences on that account. The moral effect of it upon the minds of his followers was of great value. It opened the way for their reception of the Christian faith, if any of them should be disposed to receive it. Then it changed wholly the feeling which prevailed among the Saxon soldiery, and also the Saxon chieftains, in respect to these enemies. A great deal of the bitterness of exasperation with which they had regarded them arose from the fact that they were pagans, the haters and despisers of the rites and institutions of religion. Guthrum's approaching baptism was to change all this; and Alfred, in leading him to the baptismal font, was achieving, in the estimation not only of all England, but of France and of Rome, a far greater and nobler victory than when he conquered his armies on the field of Edendune.

The various ceremonies connected with the baptism were protracted through several days. They were commenced at a place called Aulre, near Ethelney, where there was a religious establishment and priests to perform the necessary rites. The new convert was clothed in white garments—the symbol of purity, then customarily worn by candidates for baptism—and was covered with a mystic veil. They gave Guthrum a new name—a Christian, that is, a Saxon name. Converted pagans received always a new name, in those days, when baptized; and our common phrase, *the Christian name*, has arisen from the circumstance. Guthrum's Christian name was Ethelstan. Alfred was his godfather. After the baptism the whole party proceeded to a town a few miles distant, which Alfred had decided to make a royal residence, and there other ceremonies connected with the new convert's admission to the Church were performed, the whole ending with a series of great public festivities and rejoicings.

A very full and formal treaty of peace and amity was now concluded between the two sovereigns; for Guthrum was styled in the treaty a *king*, and was to hold, in the dominions assigned him to the eastward of Alfred's realm, an independent jurisdiction. He agreed, however, by this treaty, to confine himself, from that time forward, to the limits thus assigned. If the reader wishes to see what part of England

Treaty between Alfred and Guthrum. Kingdom of the latter

it was which Guthrum was thus to hold, he can easily identify it by finding upon the map the following counties, which now occupy the same territory, viz., Norfolk, Suffolk, Cambridgeshire, Essex, and part of Herefordshire. The population of all this region consisted already, in a great measure, of Danes. It was the part most easily accessible from the German Ocean, by means of the Thames and the Medway, and it had, accordingly, become the chief seat of the Northmen's power.

Guthrum not only agreed to confine himself to the limits thus marked out, but also to consider himself henceforth as Alfred's friend and ally in the event of any new bands of adventurers arriving on the coast, and to join Alfred in his endeavors to resist them. In hoping that he would fulfill this obligation, Alfred did not rely altogether on Guthrum's oaths or promises, or even on the hostages that he held. He had made it for his *interest* to fulfill them. By giving him peaceable possession of this territory, after having, by his victories, impressed him with a very high idea of his own great military resources and power, he had placed his conquered enemy under very strong inducements to be satisfied with what he now possessed, and to make common cause with Alfred in resisting the encroachments of any new marauders.

Guthrum was therefore honestly resolved on keeping his faith with his new ally; and when all these stipulations were made, and the treaties were signed, and the ceremonies of the baptism all performed, Alfred dismissed his guest, with many presents and high honors.

There is some uncertainty whether Alfred did not, in addition to the other stipulations under which he bound Guthrum, reserve to himself the superior sovereignty over Guthrum's dominions, in such a manner that Guthrum, though complimented in the treaty with the title of king, was, after all, only a sort of vice roy, holding his throne under Alfred as his liege lord. One thing is certain, that Alfred took care, in his treaty with Guthrum, to settle all the fundamental laws of both kingdoms, making them the same for both, as if he foresaw the complete and entire union which was ulti mately to take place, and wished to facilitate the accomplishment of this end by having the political and social constitution of the two states brought at once into harmony with each other.

It proved, in the end, that Guthrum was

faithful to his obligations and promises. He settled himself quietly in the dominions which the treaty assigned to him, and made no more attempts to encroach upon Alfred's realm. Whenever other parties of Danes came upon the coast, as they sometimes did, they found no favor or countenance from him. They came, in some cases, expecting his co-operation and aid; but he always refused it, and by this discouragement, as well as by open resistance, he drove many bands away, turning the tide of invasion southward into France, and other regions on the Continent. Alfred, in the mean time, gave his whole time and attention to organizing the various departments of his government, to planning and building towns, repairing and fortifying castles, opening roads, establishing courts of justice, and arranging and setting in operation the complicated machinery necessary in the working of a well-conducted social state. The nature and operation of some of his plans will be described more fully in the next chapter.

In concluding this chapter, we will add, that notwithstanding his victory over Guthrum, and Guthrum's subsequent good faith, Alfred never enjoyed an absolute peace, but during the whole

| Continued trouble from the Danes. | Alfred's character |

remainder of his reign was more or less molested with parties of Northmen, who came, from time to time, to land on English shores, and who met sometimes with partial and temporary success in their depredations. The most serious of these attempts occurred near the close of Alfred's life, and will be hereafter described.

The generosity and the nobleness of mind which Alfred manifested in his treatment of Guthrum made a great impression upon mankind at the time, and have done a great deal to elevate the character of our hero in every subsequent age. All admire such generosity in others, however slow they may be to practice it themselves. It seems a very easy virtue when we look upon an exhibition of it like this, where we feel no special resentments ourselves against the person thus nobly forgiven. We find it, however, a very hard virtue to practice, when a case occurs requiring the exercise of it toward a person who has done *us* an injury. Let those who think that in Alfred's situation they should have acted as he did, look around upon the circle of their acquaintance, and see whether it is easy for them to pursue a similar course toward their personal enemies—those who have

Alfred's kindness of heart.   *The child in the eagle's nest*

thwarted and circumvented them in their plans, or slandered them, or treated them with insult and injury. By observing how hard it is to change our own resentments to feelings of forgiveness and good will, we can the better appreciate Alfred's treatment of Guthrum.

Alfred was famed during all his life for the kindness of his heart, and a thousand stories were told in his day of his interpositions to right the wronged, to relieve the distressed, to comfort the afflicted, and to befriend the unhappy. On one occasion, as it is said, when he was hunting in a wood, he heard the piteous cries of a child, which seemed to come from the air above his head. It was found, after much looking and listening, that the sounds proceeded from an eagle's nest upon the top of a lofty tree. On climbing to the nest, they found the child within, screaming with pain and terror. The eagle had carried it there in its talons for a prey. Alfred brought down the boy, and, after making fruitless inquiries to find its father and mother, adopted him for his own son, gave him a good education, and provided for him well in his future life. The story was all, very probably, a fabrication; but the characters of men are sometimes very strikingly indicated by the kind of stories that are *invented* concerning them.

PORTRAIT OF ALFRED.

Chapter XI.
Character of Alfred's Reign.

PERHAPS the chief aspect in which King Alfred's character has attracted the attention of mankind, is in the spirit of humanity and benevolence which he manifested, and in the efforts which he made to cultivate the arts of peace, and to promote the intellectual and social welfare of his people, notwithstanding the warlike habits to which he was accustomed in his early years, and the warlike influences which surrounded him during all his life. Every thing in the outward circumstances in which he was placed tended to make him a mere military hero. He saw, however, the superior greatness and glory of the work of laying the foundations of an extended and permanent power, by arranging in the best possible manner the internal organization of the social state. He saw that intelligence, order, justice, and system, prevailing in and governing the institutions of a country, constitute the true elements of its greatness, and he acted accordingly

Character of the materials upon which Alfred operated.

It is true, he had good materials to work with He had the Anglo-Saxon race to act upon at the time, a race capable of appreciating and entering into his plans; and he has had the same race to carry them on, for the ten centuries which have elapsed since he laid his foundations. As no other race of men but Anglo-Saxons could have produced an Alfred, so, probably, no other race could have carried out such plans as Alfred formed. It is a race which has always been distinguished, like Alfred their great prototype and model, for a certain cool and intrepid energy in war, combined with and surpassed by the industry, the system, the efficiency, and the perseverance with which they pursue and perfect all the arts of peace. They systematize every thing. They arrange—they organize. Every thing in their hands takes form, and advances to continual improvement Even while the rest of the world remain inert, they are active. When the arts and improvements of life are stationary among other nations, they are always advancing with *them* It is a people that is always making new discoveries, pressing forward to new enterprises, framing new laws, constituting new combinations and developing new powers; until now

The difficulties with which Alfred had to contend.

after the lapse of a thousand years, the little island feeds and clothes, directly or indirectly, a very large portion of the human race, and directs, in a great measure, the politics of the world.

Whether Alfred reasoned upon the capacities of the people whom he ruled, and foresaw their future power, or whether he only followed the simple impulses of his own nature in the plans which he formed and the measures which he adopted, we can not know; but we know that, in fact, he devoted his chief attention, during all the years of his reign, to perfecting in the highest degree the internal organization of his realm, considered as a great social community. His people were in a very rude, and, in fact, almost half-savage state when he commenced his career. He had every thing to do, and yet he seems to have had no favorable opportunities for doing any thing.

In the first place, his time and attention were distracted, during his whole reign, by continued difficulties and contentions with various hordes of Danes, even after his peace with Guthrum These troubles, and the military preparations and movements to which they would naturally give rise, would seem to have been sufficient to

Alfred's sufferings from disease. His patience.

have occupied fully all the powers of his mind, and to have prevented him from doing any thing effectual for the internal improvement of his kingdom.

Then, besides, there was another difficulty with which Alfred had to contend, which one might have supposed would have paralyzed all his energies. He suffered all his life from some mysterious and painful internal disease, the nature of which, precisely, is not known, as the allusions to it, though very frequent throughout his life, are very general, and the physicians of the day, who probably were not very skillful, could not determine what it was, or do any thing effectual to relieve it. The disease, whatever it may have been, was a source of continual uneasiness, and sometimes of extreme and terrible suffering. Alfred bore all the pain which it caused him with exemplary patience; and, though he could not always resist the tendency to discouragement and depression with which the perpetual presence of such a torment wears upon the soul, he did not allow it to diminish his exertions, or suspend, at any time, the ceaseless activity with which he labored for the welfare of the people of his realm.

Alfred attached great importance to the edu-

| Alfred's interest in learning. | Asser, the Welsh bishop |

cation of his people. It was not possible, in those days, to educate the mass, for there were no books, and no means of producing them in sufficient numbers to supply any general demand. Books, in those days, were extremely costly, as they had all to be written laboriously by hand. The great mass of the population, therefore, who were engaged in the daily toil of cultivating the land, were necessarily left in ignorance; but Alfred made every effort in his power to awaken a love for learning and the arts among the higher classes. He set them, in fact, an efficient example in his own case, by pressing forward diligently in his own studies, even in the busiest periods of his reign. The spirit and manner in which he did this are well illustrated by the plan he pursued in studying Latin. It was this:

He had a friend in his court, a man of great literary attainments and great piety, whose name was Asser. Asser was a bishop in Wales when Alfred first heard of his fame as a man of learning and abilities, and Alfred sent for him to come to his court and make him a visit. Alfred was very much pleased with what he saw of Asser at this interview, and proposed to him to leave his preferments in Wales, which

Alfred's proposals to Asser.   *Asser's acceptance*

were numerous and important, and come into his kingdom, and he would give him greater preferments there. Asser hesitated. Alfred then proposed to him to spend six months every year in England, and the remaining six in Wales. Asser said that he could not give an answer even to this proposal till he had returned home and consulted with the monks and other clergy under his charge there. He would, however, he said, at least come back and see Alfred again within the next six months, and give him his final answer. Then, after having spent four days in Alfred's court, he went away.

The six months passed away and he did not return. Alfred sent a messenger into Wales to ascertain the reason. The messenger found that Asser was sick. His friends, however, had advised that he should accede to Alfred's proposal to spend six months of the year in England, as they thought that by that means, through his influence with Alfred, he would be the better able to protect and advance the interests of their monasteries and establishments in Wales. So Asser went to England, and became during six months in the year Alfred's constant friend and teacher. In the course of time, Alfred placed him at the head of some of

Alfred and Asser. *Alfred's Latin book.*

the most important establishments and ecclesiastical charges in England.

One day—it was eight or nine years after Alfred's victory over Guthrum and settlement of the kingdom—the king and Asser were engaged in conversation in the royal apartments, and Asser quoted some Latin phrase with which, on its being explained, Alfred was very much pleased, and he asked Asser to write it down for him in his book. So saying, he took from his pocket a little book of prayers and other pieces of devotion, which he was accustomed to carry with him for daily use. It was, of course, in manuscript. Asser looked over it to find a space where he could write the Latin quotation, but there was no convenient vacancy. He then proposed to Alfred that he should make for him another small book, expressly for Latin quotations, with explanations of their meaning, if Alfred chose to make them, in the Anglo-Saxon tongue. Alfred highly approved of this suggestion. The bishop prepared the little parchment volume, and it became gradually filled with passages of Scripture, in Latin, and striking sentiments, briefly and tersely expressed, extracted from the writings of the Roman poets or of the fathers of the Church. Alfred wrote

Alfred becomes an author.   *Printing and circulation of books.*

opposite to each quotation its meaning, expressed in his own language; and as he made the book his constant companion, and studied it continually, taking great interest in adding to its stores, it was the means of communicating to him soon a very considerable knowledge of the language, and was the foundation of that extensive acquaintance with it which he subsequently acquired.

Alfred made great efforts to promote in every way the intellectual progress and improvement of his people. He wrote and translated books, which were published so far as it was possible to publish books in those days, that is, by having a moderate number of copies transcribed and circulated among those who could read them. Such copies were generally deposited at monasteries, and abbeys, and other such places, where learned men were accustomed to assemble. These writings of Alfred exerted a wide influence during his day. They remained in manuscript until the art of printing was invented, when many of them were printed; others remain in manuscript in the various museums of England, where visitors look at them as curiosities, all worn and corroded as they are, and almost illegible by time. These books, though

Influence of Alfred's writings. Founding of the University of Oxford.

they exerted great influence at the time when they were written, are of little interest or value now. They express ideas in morals and philosophy, some of which have become so universally diffused as to be commonplace at the present day, while others would now be discarded, as not in harmony with the ideas or the philosophy of the times.

One of the greatest and most important of the measures which Alfred adopted for the intellectual improvement of his people was the founding of the great University of Oxford. Oxford was Alfred's residence and capital during a considerable part of his reign. It is situated on the Thames, in the bosom of a delightful valley, where it calmly reposes in the midst of fields and meadows as verdant and beautiful as the imagination can conceive. There was a monastery at Oxford before Alfred's day, and for many centuries after his time acts of endowment were passed and charters granted, some of which were perhaps of greater importance than those which emanated from Alfred himself. Thus some carry back the history of this famous university beyond Alfred's time; others consider that the true origin of the present establishment should be assigned to a later date than his day. Alfred certainly adopted very important measures at Oxford for organizing and establishing schools of instruction and assembling learned men there from various parts of the world, so that he soon made it a great center and seat of learning, and mankind have been consequently inclined to award to him the honor of having laid the foundations of the vast superstructure which has since grown up on that consecrated spot. Oxford is now a city of ancient and venerable colleges. Its silent streets; its grand quadrangles; its churches, and chapels, and libraries; its secluded walks; its magnificent, though old and crumbling architecture, make it, even to the passing traveler, one of the wonders of England; and by the influence which it has exerted for the past ten centuries on the intellectual advancement of the human race, it is really one of the wonders of the world.

Alfred repaired the castles which had become dilapidated in the wars; he rebuilt the ruined cities, organized municipal governments for them, restored the monasteries, and took great pains to place men of learning and piety in charge of them. He revised the laws of the kingdom, and arranged and systematized them in the most perfect manner which was possible in times so rude

Alfred's personal character. — *Reforms and improvements.*

Alfred's personal character gave him great influence among his people, and disposed them to acquiesce readily in the vast innovations and improvements which he introduced—changes which were so radical and affected so extensively the whole structure of society, and all the customs of social life, that any ordinary sovereign would have met with great opposition in his attempt to introduce them; but Alfred possessed such a character, and proceeded in such a way in introducing his improvements and reforms, that he seems to have awakened no jealousy and to have aroused no resistance.

He was of a very calm, quiet, and placid temper of mind. The crosses and vexations which disturb and irritate ordinary men seemed never to disturb his equanimity. He was patient and forbearing, never expecting too much of those whom he employed, or resenting angrily the occasional neglects or failures in duty on their part, which he well knew must frequently occur. He was never elated by prosperity, nor made moody and morose by the turning of the tide against him. In a word, he was a philosopher, of a calm, and quiet, and happy temper.

ament. He knew well that every man in going through life, whatever his rank and station, must encounter the usual alternations of sunshine and storm. He determined that these alternations should not mar his happiness, nor disturb the repose of his soul; that he would, on the other hand, keeping all quiet within, press calmly and steadily forward in the accomplishment of the vast objects to which he felt that his life was to be given. He was, accordingly, never anxious or restless, never impatient or fretful, never excited or wild; but always calm, considerate, steady, and persevering, he infused his own spirit into all around him. They saw him governed by fixed and permanent principles of justice and of duty in all that he planned, and in every measure that he resorted to in the execution of his plans. It was plain that his great ruling motive was a true and honest desire to promote the welfare and prosperity of his people, and the internal peace, and order, and happiness of his realm without any selfish or sinister aims of his own.

In fact, it seemed as if there were no selfish or sinister ends that possessed any charms for Alfred's mind. He had no fondness or taste for luxury or pleasure, or for aggrandizing him

Alfred's solicitude for his country.   His diligence.

self in the eyes of others by pomp and parade. It is true that, as was stated in a former chapter, he was charged in early life with a tendency to some kinds of wrong indulgence; but these charges, obscure and doubtful as they were, pertained only to the earliest periods of his career, before the time of his seclusion. Through all the middle and latter portions of his life, the sole motive of his conduct seems to have been a desire to lay broad, and deep, and lasting foundations for the permanent welfare and prosperity of his realm.

It resulted from the nature of the measures which Alfred undertook to effect, that they brought upon him daily a vast amount of labor as such measures always involve a great deal of minute detail. Alfred could only accomplish this great mass of duty by means of the most unremitting industry and the most systematic and exact division of time. There were no clocks or watches in those days, and yet it was very necessary to have some plan for keeping the time, in order that his business might go on regularly, and also that the movements and operations of his large household might proceed without confusion. Alfred invented a plan. It was as follows·

He observed that the wax candles which were used in his palace and in the churches burned very regularly, and with greater or less rapidity according to their size. He ordered some experiments to be made, and finally, by means of them, he determined on the size of a candle which should burn three inches in an hour. It is said that the weight of wax which he used for each candle was twelve pennyweights, that is, but little more than half an ounce, which would make, one would suppose, a *taper* rather than a candle. There is, however, great doubt about the value of the various denominations of weight and measure, and also of money used in those days. However this may be, the candles were each a foot long, and of such size that each would burn four hours. They were divided into inches, and marked, so that each inch corresponded with a third of an hour, or twenty minutes. A large quantity of these candles were prepared, and a person in one of the chapels was appointed to keep a succession of them burning, and to ring the bells, or give the other signals, whatever they might be, by which the household was regulated, at the successive periods of time denoted by their burning.

As each of these candles was one foot long,

Working of the system. *Introduction of glass.*

and burned three inches in an hour, it follows that it would last four hours; when this time was expired, the attendant who had the apparatus in charge lighted another. There were, of course, six required for the whole twenty-four hours. The system worked very well, though there was one difficulty that occasioned some trouble in the outset, which, however, was not much to be regretted after all, since the remedying of it awakened the royal ingenuity anew, and led, in the end, to adding to Alfred's other glories the honor of being the inventor of *lanterns!*

The difficulty was, that the wind, which came in very freely in those days, even in royal residences, through the open windows, blew the flames of these horological candles about, so as to interfere quite seriously with the regularity of their burning. There was no glass for windows in those days, or, at least, very little. It had been introduced, it is said, in one instance, and that was in a monastery in the north of England. The abbot, whose name was Benedict, brought over some workmen from the Continent, where the art of making glass windows had been invented, and caused them to glaze some windows in his monastery. It was many years after this before glass came into general use even in churches, and palaces, and other costly buildings of that kind. In the mean time, windows were mere openings in stone walls, which could be closed only by shutters; and inasmuch as when closed they excluded the light as well as the air, they could ordinarily be shut only on one side of the apartment at a time—the side most exposed to the winds and storms.

Alfred accordingly found that the flame of his candles was blown by the wind, which made the wax burn irregularly; and, to remedy the evil, he contrived the plan of protecting them by thin plates of horn. Horn, when softened by hot water, can easily be cut and fashioned into any shape, and, when very thin, is almost transparent. Alfred had these thin plates of horn prepared, and set into the sides of a box made open to receive them, thus forming a rude sort of lantern, within which the time-keeping candles could burn in peace. Mankind have consequently given to King Alfred the credit of having invented lanterns.

Having thus completed his apparatus for the correct measurement of time, Alfred was enabled to be more and more systematic in the

Alfred's division of his time. — Its wisdom.

division and employment of it. One of the historians of the day relates that his plan was to give one third of the twenty-four hours to sleep and refreshment, one third to business, and the remaining third to the duties of religion. Under this last head was probably included all those duties and pursuits which, by the customs of the day, were considered as pertaining to the Church, such as study, writing, and the consideration and management of ecclesiastical affairs. These duties were performed, in those days, almost always by clerical men, and in the retirement and seclusion of monasteries, and were thus regarded as in some sense religious duties. We must conclude that Alfred classed them thus, as he was a great student and writer all his days, and there is no other place than this third head to which the duties of this nature can be assigned. Thus understood, it was a very wise and sensible division; though eight hours daily for any long period of time, appropriated to services strictly devotional, would not seem to be a wise arrangement, especially for a man in the prime of life, and in a position demanding the constant exercise of his powers in the discharge of active duties.

Thus the years of Alfred's life passed away.

Alfred's prosperity. — *Troubles from the Danes.*

his kingdom advancing steadily all the time in good government, wealth, and prosperity. The country was not, however, yet freed entirely from the calamities and troubles arising from the hostility of the Danes. Disorders continually broke out among those who had settled in the land, and, in some instances, new hordes of invaders came in. These were, however, in most instances, easily subdued, and Alfred went on with comparatively little interruption for many years, in prosecuting the arts and improvements of peace. At last, however, toward the close of his life, a famous Northman leader, named Hastings, landed in England at the head of a large force, and made, before he was expelled, a great deal of trouble. An account of this invasion will be given in the next chapter.

nvasion of Hastings.   His exploits on the Continent

Chapter XII.

The Close of Life

IT was twelve or fifteen years after Alfred's restoration to his kingdom, by means of the victory at Edendune, that the great invasion of Hastings occurred. That victory took place in the year 878. It was in the years 893–897 that Hastings and his horde of followers infested the island, and in 900 Alfred died, so that his reign ended, as it had commenced, with protracted and desperate conflicts with the Danes.

Hastings was an old and successful soldier before he came to England. He had led a wild life for many years as a sea king on the German Ocean, performing deeds which in our day entail upon the perpetrator of them the infamy of piracy and murder, but which then entitled the hero of them to a very wide-spread and honorable fame. Afterward Hastings landed upon the Continent, and pursued, for a long time, a glorious career of victory and plunder in France. In these enterprises, the tide, indeed, sometimes turned against him. On one occasion, for in-

Hastings besieged in a church. *The place of landing*

stance, he found himself obliged to give way before his enemies, and he retreated to a church, which he seized and fortified, making it his castle until a more favorable aspect of his affairs enabled him to issue forth from this retreat and take the field again. Still he was generally very successful in his enterprises; his terrible ferocity, and that of his savage followers, were dreaded in every part of the civilized world.

Hastings had made one previous invasion of England; but Guthrum, faithful to his covenants with Alfred, repulsed him. But Guthrum was now dead, and Alfred had to contend against his formidable enemy alone.

Hastings selected a point on the southern coast of England for his landing. Guthrum's Danes still continued to occupy the eastern part of England, and Hastings went round on the southern coast until he got beyond their boundaries, as if he wished to avoid doing any thing directly to awaken their hostility. Guthrum himself, while he lived, had evinced a determination to oppose Hastings's plans of invasion. Hastings did not know, now that Guthrum was dead, whether his successors would oppose him or not. He determined, at all events, to respect their territory, and so he passed along

HASTINGS BESIEGED IN THE CHURCH

Forces of the Danes. Romney Marshes.

on the southern shore of England till he was beyond their limits, and then prepared to land.

He had assembled a large force of his own, and he was joined, in addition to them, by many adventurers who came out to attach themselves to his expedition from the bays, and islands, and harbors which he passed on his way His fleet amounted at least to two hundred and fifty vessels. They arrived, at length, at a part of the coast where there extends a vast tract of low and swampy land, which was then a wild and dismal morass. This tract, which is known in modern times by the name of the Romney Marshes, is of enormous extent, containing, as it does, fifty thousand acres. It is now reclaimed, and is defended by a broad and well-constructed dike from the inroads of the sea. In Hastings's time it was a vast waste of bogs and mire, utterly impassable except by means of a river, which, meandering sluggishly through the tangled wilderness of weeds and bushes in a deep, black stream, found an outlet at last into the sea.

Hastings took his vessels into this river, and, following its turnings for some miles, he conducted them at last to a place where he found more solid ground to land upon. But this ground, though solid, was almost as wild and solitary as the morass. It was a forest of vast extent, which showed no signs of human occupancy, except that the peasants who lived in the surrounding regions had come down to the lowest point accessible, and were building a rude fortification there. Hastings attacked them and drove them away. Then, advancing a little further, until he found an advantageous position, he built a strong fortress himself and established his army within its lines.

His next measure was to land another force near the mouth of the Thames, and bring them to the country, until he found a strong position where he could intrench and fortify the second division as he had done the first. These two positions were but a short distance from each other. He made them the combined center of his operations, going from them in all directions in plundering excursions. Alfred soon raised an army and advanced to attack him; and these operations were the commencement of a long and tedious war.

A detailed description of the events of this war, the marches and countermarches, the battles and sieges, the various success, first of one party and then of the other, given historically

Cautious policy of Alfred. | Negotiations.

in the order of time, would be as tedious to read as the war itself was to endure. Alfred was very cautious in all his operations, preferring rather to trust to the plan of wearing out the enemy by cutting off their resources and hemming them constantly in, than to incur the risk of great decisive battles. In fact, watchfulness, caution, and delay are generally the policy of the invaded when a powerful force has succeeded in establishing itself among them; while, on the other hand, the hope of *invaders* lies ordinarily in prompt and decided action Alfred was well aware of this, and made all his arrangements with a view to cutting off Hastings's supplies, shutting him up into as narrow a compass as possible, heading him off in all his predatory excursions, intercepting all detachments, and thus reducing him at length to the necessity of surrender.

At one time, soon after the war began, Hastings, true to the character of his nation for treachery and stratagem, pretended that he was ready to surrender, and opened a negotiation for this purpose. He agreed to leave the kingdom if Alfred would allow him to depart peaceably, and also, which was a point of great importance in Alfred's estimation, to have his two sons baptized. While, however, these negotiations were going on between the two camps, Alfred suddenly found that the main body of Hastings's army had stolen away in the rear, and were marching off by stealth to another part of the country. The negotiations were, of course, immediately abandoned, and Alfred set off with all his forces in full pursuit. All hopes of peace were given up, and the usual series of sieges, manœuverings, battles, and retreats was resumed again.

On one occasion Alfred succeeded in taking possession of Hastings's camp, when he had left it in security, as he supposed, to go off for a time by sea on an expedition. Alfred's soldiers found Hastings's wife and children in the camp, and took them prisoners. They sent the terrified captives to Alfred, to suffer, as they supposed, the long and cruel confinement or the violent death to which the usages of those days consigned such unhappy prisoners. Alfred baptized the children, and then sent them, with their mother, loaded with presents and proofs of kindness, back to Hastings again.

This generosity made no impression upon the heart of Hastings, or, at least, it produced no effect upon his conduct. He continued the war as energetically as ever. Months passed away and new re-enforcements arrived, until at length he felt strong enough to undertake an excursion into the very heart of the country. He moved on for a time with triumphant success; but this very success was soon the means of turning the current against him again. It aroused the whole country through which he was passing. The inhabitants flocked to arms. They assembled at every rallying point, and, drawing up on all sides nearer and nearer to Hastings's army, they finally stopped his march, and forced him to call all his forces in, and intrench himself in the first place of retreat that he could find. Thus his very success was the means of turning his good fortune into disaster.

And then, in the same way, the success of Alfred and the Saxons soon brought disaster upon them too, in their turn; for, after succeeding in shutting Hastings closely in, and cutting off his supplies of food, they maintained their watch and ward over their imprisoned enemies so closely as to reduce them to extreme distress—a distress and suffering which they thought would end in their complete and absolute submission. Instead of ending thus, however, it aroused them to desperation. Under

Desperate sally of the Danes.   **They sail up the Thames**

the influence of the phrensy which such hopeless sufferings produce in characters like theirs, they burst out one day from the place of their confinement, and, after a terrible conflict, which choked up a river which they had to pass with dead bodies and dyed its waters with blood, the great body of the starving desperadoes made their escape, and, in a wild and furious excitement, half a triumph and half a retreat, they went back to the eastern coast of the island, where they found secure places of refuge to receive them.

In the course of the subsequent campaigns, a party of the Danes came up the River Thames with a fleet of their vessels, and an account is given by some of the ancient historians of a measure which Alfred resorted to to entrap them, which would seem to be scarcely credible. The account is, that he *altered the course of the river* by digging new channels for it, so as to leave the vessels all aground, when, of course, they became helpless, and fell an easy prey to the attacks of their enemies. This is, at least, a very improbable statement, for a river like the Thames occupies always the lowest channel of the land through which it passes to the sea. Besides, such a river, in order that it should be possible for vessels to ascend it from the ocean. must have the surface of its water very near the level of the surface of the ocean. There can, therefore, be no place to which such waters could be drawn off, unless into a valley below the level of the sea. All such valleys, whenever they exist in the interior of a country, necessarily get filled with water from brooks and rains, and so become lakes or inland seas It is probable, therefore, that it was some other operation which Alfred performed to imprison the hostile vessels in the river, more possible in its own nature than the drawing off of the waters of the Thames from their ancient bed.

Year after year passed on, and, though neither the Saxons nor the Danes gained any very permanent and decisive victories, the invaders were gradually losing ground, being driven from one intrenchment and one stronghold to another, until, at last, their only places of refuge were their ships, and the harbors along the margin of the sea. Alfred followed on and occupied the country as fast as the enemy was driven away; and when, at last, they began to seek refuge in their ships, he advanced to the shore, and began to form plans for building ships, and manning and equipping a fleet, to pursue his retiring en-

Alfred builds a fleet.   *It sails for the Isle of Wight*

emies upon their own element. In this undertaking, he proceeded in the same calm, deliberate, and effectual manner, as in all his preceding measures. He built his vessels with great care He made them twice as long as those of the Danes, and planned them so as to make them more steady, more safe, and capable of carrying a crew of rowers so numerous as to be more active and swift than the vessels of the enemy.

When these naval preparations were made, Alfred began to look out for an object of attack on which he could put their efficiency to the test. He soon heard of a fleet of the Northmen's vessels on the coast of the Isle of Wight, and he sent a fleet of his own ships to attack them. He charged the commander of this fleet to be sparing of life, but to capture the ships and take the men, bringing as many as possible to him unharmed.

There were nine of the English vessels, and when they reached the Isle of Wight they found six vessels of the Danes in a harbor there Three of these Danish vessels were afloat, and came out boldly to attack Alfred's armament. The other three were upon the shore, where they had been left by the tide, and were, of course, disabled and defenseless until the water

| Naval battle. | Discomfiture of the Saxons |

should rise and float them again. Under these circumstances, it would seem that the victory for Alfred's fleet would have been easy and sure; and at first the result was, in fact, in Alfred's favor. Of the three ships that came out to meet him, two were captured, and one escaped, with only five men left on board of it alive. The Saxon ships, after thus disposing of the three living and moving enemies, pushed boldly into the harbor to attack those which were lying lifeless on the sands. They found, however, that, though successful in the encounter with the active and the powerful, they were destined to disaster and defeat in approaching the defenseless and weak. They got aground themselves in approaching the shoals on which the vessels of their enemies were lying. The tide receded and left three of the vessels on the sands, and kept the rest so separated and so embarrassed by the difficulties and dangers of their situation as to expose the whole force to the most imminent danger. There was a fierce contest in boats and on the shore. Both parties suffered very severely; and, finally, the Danes, getting first released, made their escape and put to sea.

Notwithstanding this partial discomfiture,

Hastings expelled.   Alfred devotes himself to peaceful avocations

Alfred soon succeeded in driving the ships of the Danes off his coast, and in thus completing the deliverance of his country. Hastings himself went to France, where he spent the remainder of his days in some territories which he had previously conquered, enjoying, while he continued to live, and for many ages afterward, a very extended and very honorable fame. Such exploits as those which he had performed conferred, in those days, upon the hero who performed them, a very high distinction, the luster of which seems not to have been at all tarnished in the opinions of mankind by any ideas of the violence and wrong which the commission of such deeds involved.

Alfred's dominions were now left once more in peace, and he himself resumed again his former avocations. But a very short period of his life, however, now remained. Hastings was finally expelled from England about 897. In 900 or 901 Alfred died. The interval was spent in the same earnest and devoted efforts to promote the welfare and prosperity of his kingdom that his life had exhibited before the war He was engaged diligently and industriously in repairing injuries, redressing grievances, and rectifying every thing that was wrong

Administration of justice. *Alfred's children.*

He exacted rigid impartiality in all the courts of justice; he held public servants of every rank and station to a strict accountability; and in all the colleges, and monasteries, and ecclesiastical establishments of every kind, he corrected all abuses, and enforced a rigid discipline, faithfully extirpating from every lurking place all semblance of immorality or vice. He did these things, too, with so much kindness and consideration for all concerned, and was actuated in all he did so unquestionably by an honest and sincere desire to fulfill his duty to his people and to God, that nobody opposed him. The good considered him their champion, the indifferent readily caught a portion of his spirit and wished him success, while the wicked were silenced if they were not changed.

Alfred's children had grown up to maturity, and seemed to inherit, in some degree, their father's character. He had a daughter, named Æthelfleda, who was married to a prince of Mercia, and who was famed all over England for the superiority of her mental powers, her accomplishments, and her moral worth. The name of his oldest son was Edward; he was to succeed Alfred on the throne, and it was a source now of great satisfaction to the king to find this son emulating his virtues, and preparing for an honorable and prosperous reign. Alfred had warning, in the progress of his disease, of the approach of his end. When he found that the time was near at hand, he called his son Edward to his side, and gave him these his farewell counsels, which express in few words the principles and motives by which his own life had been so fully governed.

"Thou, my dear son, set thee now beside me, and I will deliver thee true instructions. I feel that my hour is coming. My strength is gone; my countenance is wasted and pale. My days are almost ended. We must now part I go to another world, and thou art to be left alone in the possession of all that I have thus far held. I pray thee, my dear child, to be a father to thy people. Be the children's father and the widow's friend. Comfort the poor, protect and shelter the weak, and, with all thy might, right that which is wrong. And, my son, govern *thyself* by *law*. Then shall the Lord love thee, and God himself shall be thy reward. Call thou upon him to advise thee in all thy need, and he shall help thee to compass all thy desires."

Alfred's death and burial. Lasting honor to his memory.

Alfred was fifty-two years of age when he died. His death was universally lamented The body was interred in the great cathedral at Winchester. The kingdom passed peacefully and prosperously to his son, and the arrangements which Alfred had spent his life in framing and carrying into effect, soon began to work out their happy results. The constructions which he founded stand to the present day, strengthened and extended rather than impaired by the hand of time; and his memory, as their founder, will be honored as long as any remembrance of the past shall endure among the minds of men.

Chapter XIII.
The Sequel.

THE romantic story of Godwin forms the sequel to the history of Alfred, leading us onward, as it does, toward the next great era in English history, that of William the Conqueror.

Although, as we have seen in the last chapter, the immediate effects of Alfred's measures was to re-establish peace and order in his kingdom, and although the institutions which he founded have continued to expand and develop themselves down to the present day, still it must not be supposed that the power and prosperity of his kingdom and of the Saxon dynasty continued wholly uninterrupted after his death. Contentions and struggles between the two great races of Saxons and Danes continued for some centuries to agitate the island. The particular details of these contentions have in these days, in a great measure, lost their interest for all but professed historical scholars. It is only the history of great leading events and the lives of really extraordinary men, in the annals of early ages, which can now attract the general attention even of cultivated minds. The vast movements which have occurred and are occurring in the history of mankind in the present century, throw every thing except what is really striking and important in early history into the shade.

The era which comes next in the order of time to that of Alfred in the course of English history, as worthy to arrest general attention, is, as we have already said, that of William the Conqueror. The life of this sovereign forms the subject of a separate volume of this series. He lived two centuries after Alfred's day; and although, for the reasons above given, a full chronological narration of the contentions between the Saxon and Danish lines of kings which took place during this interval would be of little interest or value, some general knowledge of the state of the kingdom at this time is important, and may best be communicated in connection with the story of Godwin.

Godwin was by birth a Saxon peasant, of Warwickshire. At the time when he arrived at manhood, and was tending his father's flocks and herds like other peasants' sons, the Saxons and the Danes were at war. It seems that one

| Ethelred. | His marriage. | Canute the Dane |

of Alfred's descendants, named Ethelred, displeased his people by his misgovernment, and was obliged to retire from England. He went across the Channel, and married there the sister of a Norman chief named Richard. Her name was Emma. Ethelred hoped by this alliance to obtain Richard's assistance in enabling him to recover his kingdom. The Danish population, however, took advantage of his absence to put one of their own princes upon the throne. His name was Canute. He figures in English history, accordingly, among the other English kings, as Canute the Dane, that appellation being given him to mark the distinction of his origin in respect to the kings who preceded and followed him, as they were generally of the Saxon line.

It was this Canute of whom the famous story is told that, in order to rebuke his flatterers, who, in extolling his grandeur and power, had represented to him that even the elements were subservient to his will, he took his stand upon the sea-shore when the tide was coming in, with his flatterers by his side, and commanded the rising waves not to approach his royal feet. He kept his sycophantic courtiers in this ridiculous position until the encroaching waters drove them away, and then dismissed them overwhelmed

War between Ethelred and Canuta.   *Death of Ethelred*

with confusion. The story is told in a thousand different ways, and with a great variety of different embellishments, according to the fancy of the several narrators; all that there is now any positive evidence for believing, however, is, that probably some simple incident of the kind occurred, out of which the stories have grown.

Canute did not hold his kingdom in peace. Ethelred sent his son across the Channel into England to negotiate with the Anglo-Saxon powers for his own restoration to the throne. An arrangement was accordingly made with them, and Ethelred returned, and a violent civil war immediately ensued between Ethelred and the Anglo-Saxons on the one hand, and Canute and the Danes on the other. At length Ethelred fell, and his son Edmund, who was at the time of his death one of his generals, succeeded him. Emma and his two other sons had been left in Normandy. Edmund carried on the war against Canute with great energy. One of his battles was fought in the county of Warwick, in the heart of England, where the peasant Godwir lived. In this battle the Danes were defeated, and the discomfited generals fled in all directions from the field wherever they saw the readiest hope of concealment or safety. One of them, named Ulf,* took a by-way, which led him in the direction of Godwin's father's farm.

Night came on, and he lost his way in a wood. Men, when flying under such circumstances from a field of battle, avoid always the public roads, and seek concealment in unfrequented paths, where they easily get bewildered and lost. Ulf wandered about all night in the forest, and when the morning came he found himself exhausted with fatigue, anxiety, and hunger, certain to perish unless he could find some succor, and yet dreading the danger of being recognized as a Danish fugitive if he were to be discovered by any of the Saxon inhabitants of the land. At length he heard the shouts of a peasant who was coming along a solitary pathway through the wood, driving a herd to their pasture. Ulf would gladly have avoided him if he could have gone on without succor or help. His plan was to find his way to the Severn, where some Danish ships were lying, in hopes of a refuge on board of them. But he was exhausted with hunger and fatigue, and utterly bewildered and lost; so he was compelled to go forward, and take the risk of accosting the Saxon stranger.

He accordingly went up to him, and asked

* Pronounced *Oolf*

him his name. Godwin told him his name, and the name of his father, who lived, he said, at a little distance in the wood. While he was answering the question, he gazed very earnestly at the stranger, and then told him that he perceived that he was a Dane—a fugitive, he supposed, from the battle. Ulf, thus finding that he could not be concealed, begged Godwin not to betray him. He acknowledged that he was a Dane, and that he had made his escape from the battle, and he wished, he said, to find his way to the Danish ships in the Severn. He begged Godwin to conduct him there. Godwin replied by saying that it was unreasonable and absurd for a Dane to expect guidance and protection from a Saxon.

Ulf offered Godwin all sorts of rewards if he would leave his herd and conduct him to a place of safety. Godwin said that the attempt, were he to make it, would endanger his own life without saving that of the fugitive. The country, he said, was all in arms. The peasantry, emboldened by the late victory obtained by the Saxon army, were every where rising; and although it was not far to the Severn, yet to attempt to reach the river while the country was in such a state of excitement would be a desperate undertaking. They would almost certainly be intercepted; and, if intercepted, their exasperated captors would show no mercy, Godwin said, either to him or to his guide.

Among the other inducements which Ulf offered to Godwin was a valuable gold ring, which he took from his finger, and which, he said, should be his if he would consent to be his guide. Godwin took the ring into his hand, examined it with much apparent curiosity, and seemed to hesitate. At length he yielded; though he seems to have been induced to yield, not by the value of the offered gift, but by compassion for the urgency of the distress which the offer of it indicated, for he put the ring back into Ulf's hand, saying that he would not take any thing from him, but he would try to save him.

Instead, however, of undertaking the apparently hopeless enterprise of conducting Ulf to the Severn, he took him to his father's cottage and concealed him there. During the day they formed plans for journeying together, not to the ships in the Severn, but to the Danish camp. They were to set forth as soon as it was dark. When the evening came and all was ready, and they were about to commence their dangerous journey, the old peasant, Godwin's father, with an anxious countenance and manner, gave Ulf this solemn charge:

"This is my *only* son. In going forth to guide you under these circumstances, he puts his life at stake, trusting to your honor. He can not return to me again, as there will be no more safety for him among his own countrymen after having once been a guide for you. When, therefore, you reach the camp, present my son to your king, and ask him to receive him into his service. He can not come again to me." Ulf promised very earnestly to do all this and much more for his protector; and then bidding the father farewell, and leaving him in his solitude, the two adventurers sallied forth into the dark forest and went their way.

After various adventures, they reached the camp of the Danes in safety. Ulf faithfully fulfilled the promises that he had made. He introduced Godwin to the king, and the king was so much pleased with the story of his general's escape, and so impressed with the marks of capacity and talent which the young Saxon manifested, that he gave Godwin immediately a military command in his army. In fact, a young man who could eave his home and his father, and abandon the cause of his countrymen forever under such circumstances, must have had something besides generosity toward a fugitive enemy to impel him. Godwin was soon found to possess a large portion of that peculiar spirit which constitutes a soldier. He was ambitious, stern, energetic, and always successful. He rose rapidly in influence and rank, and in the course of a few years, during which King Canute triumphed wholly over his Saxon enemies, and established his dominion over almost the whole realm, he was promoted to the rank of a king, and ruled, second only to Canute himself, over the kingdom of Wessex one of the most important divisions of Canute's empire. Here he lived and reigned in peace and prosperity for many years. He was married, and he had a daughter named Edith, who was as gentle and lovely as her father was terrible and stern. They said that Edith sprung from Godwin like a rose from its stem of thorns.

A writer who lived in those days, and recorded the occurrences of the times, says that, when he was a boy, his father was employed in some way in Godwin's palace, and that in going to and from school he was often met by Edith, who was walking, attended by her maid. On

Edith's gentleness and kindness. — *Conquests of Canute.*

such occasions Edith would stop him, he said, and question him about his studies, his grammar, his logic, and his verses; and she would often draw him into an argument on those subtle points of disputation which attracted so much attention in those days. Then she would commend him for his attention and progress, and order her woman to make him a present of some money. In a word, Edith was so gentle and kind, and took so cordial an interest in whatever concerned the welfare and happiness of those around her, that she was universally beloved. She became in the end, as we shall see in due time, the English queen.

In the mean time, while Godwin was governing, as vicegerent, the province which Canute had assigned him, Canute himself extended his own dominion far and wide, reducing first all England under his sway, and then extending his conquests to the Continent. Edmund, the Saxon king, was dead. His brothers Edward and Alfred, the two remaining sons of Ethelred, were with their mother in Normandy. They, of course, represented the Saxon line. The Saxon portion of Canute's kingdom would of course look to them as their future leaders. Under these circumstances, Canute conceived the idea

Canute marries Emma. — Policy of this act

of propitiating the Saxon portion of the population, and combining, so far as was possible, the claims of the two lines, by making the widow Emma his own wife. He made the proposal to her, and she accepted it, pleased with the idea of being once more a queen. She came to England, and they were married. In process of time they had a son, who was named Hardicanute, which means Canute *the strong*.

Canute now felt that his kingdom was secure; and he hoped, by making Hardicanute his heir, to perpetuate the dominion in his own family. It is true that he had older children, whom the Danes might look upon as more properly his heirs; and Emma had also two older children. the sons of Ethelred, in Normandy. These the *Saxons* would be likely to consider as the rightful heirs to the throne. There was danger, therefore, that at his death parties would again be formed, and the civil wars break out anew Canute and Emma therefore seem to have acted wisely, and to have done all that the nature of the case admitted to prevent a renewal of these dreadful struggles, by concentrating their combined influence in favor of Hardicanute, who, though not absolutely the heir to either line, still combined, in some degree, the claims of both of them. Canute also did all in his power to propitiate his Anglo-Saxon subjects. He devoted himself to promoting the welfare of the kingdom in every way. He built towns, he constructed roads, he repaired and endowed the churches. He became a very zealous Christian, evincing the ardor of his piety, whether real or pretended, by all the forms and indications common in those days. Finally, to crown all, he went on a pilgrimage to Rome. He set out on this journey with great pomp and parade, and attended by a large retinue, and yet still strictly like a pilgrim. He walked, and carried a wallet on his back, and a long pilgrim's staff in his hand. This pilgrimage, at the time when it occurred, filled the world with its fame.

At length King Canute died, and then, unfortunately, it proved that all his seemingly wise precautions against the recurrence of civil wars were taken in vain. It happened that Hardicanute, whom he had intended should succeed him, was in Denmark at the time of his father's death. Godwin, however, proclaimed him king, and attempted to establish his authority, and to make Emma a sort of regent, to govern in his name until he could be brought home. The Danish chieftains, on the other hand, elected and proclaimed one of Canute's older sons, whose name was Harold ;* and they succeeded in carrying a large part of the country in his favor. Godwin then summoned Emma to join him in the west with such forces as she could command, and both parties prepared for war.

Then ensued one of those scenes of terror and suffering which war, and sometimes the mere fear of war, brings often in its train. It was expected that the first outbreak of hostilities would be in the interior of England, near the banks of the Thames, and the inhabitants of the whole region were seized with apprehensions and fears, which spread rapidly, increased by the influence of sympathy, and excited more and more every day by a thousand groundless rumors, until the whole region was thrown into a state of uncontrollable panic and confusion. The inhabitants abandoned their dwellings, and fled in dismay into the eastern part of the island, to seek refuge among the fens and marshes of Lincolnshire, and of the other counties around. Here, as has been already stated in a previous chapter when describing the Abbey of Croyland, were a great many monasteries, and convents.

* Spelled sometimes Herald.

The fugitives in the Lincolnshire fens.   *Alarm of the monks.*

and hermitages, and other religious establishments, filled with monks and nuns. The wretched fugitives from the expected scene of war crowded into this region, besieging the doors of the abbeys and monasteries to beg for shelter or food, or protection. Some built huts among the willow woods which grew in the fens; others encamped at the road-sides, or under the monastery walls, wherever they could find the semblance of shelter. They presented, of course, a piteous spectacle—men infirm with sickness or age, or exhausted with anxiety and fatigue; children harassed and way-worn; and helpless mothers, with still more helpless babes at their breasts. The monks, instead of being moved to compassion by the sight of these unhappy sufferers, were only alarmed on their own account at such an inundation of misery. They feared that they should be overwhelmed themselves. Those whose establishments were large and strong, barred their doors against the suppliants, and the hermits, who lived alone in detached and separate solitudes, abandoned their osier huts, and fled themselves to seek some place more safe from such intrusions.

And yet, after all, the whole scene was only a false alarm. Men acting in a panic are al-

24—17

most always running into the ills which they think they shun. The war did not break out on the banks of the Thames at all. Hardicanute, deterred, perhaps, by the extent of the support which the claims of Harold were receiving, did not venture to come to England, and Emma and Godwin, and those who would have taken their side, having no royal head to lead them, gave up their opposition, and acquiesced in Harold's reign. The fugitives in the marshes and fens returned to their homes; the country became tranquil; Godwin held his province as a sort of lieutenant general of Harold's kingdom, and Emma herself joined his court in London, where she lived with him ostensibly on very friendly terms.

Still, her mind was ill at ease. Harold, though the son of her husband, was not her own son, and the ambitious spirit which led her to marry for her second husband her first husband's rival and enemy, that she might be a second time a queen, naturally made her desire that one of her own offspring, either on the Danish or the Saxon side, should inherit the kingdom; for the reader must not forget that Emma, besides being the mother of Hardicanute by her second husband Canute, the Danish sovereign, was also the mother of Edward and Alfred by her first husband Ethelred, of the Anglo-Saxon line, and that these two sons were in Normandy now. The family connection will be more apparent to the eye by the following scheme:

Ethelred the Saxon.	Emma.	Canute the Dane.
Edward. Alfred.		Hardicanute.

Harold was the son of Canute by a former marriage. Emma, of course, felt no maternal interest in him, and though compelled by circumstances to acquiesce for a time in his possession of the kingdom, her thoughts were continually with her own sons; and since the attempt to bring Hardicanute to the throne had failed, she began to turn her attention toward her Norman children.

After scheming for a time, she wrote letters to them, proposing that they should come to England. She represented to them that the Anglo-Saxon portion of the people were ill at ease under Harold's dominion, and would gladly embrace any opportunity of having a Saxon king. She had no doubt, she said, that if one of them were to appear in England and claim the throne, the people would rise in mass to support him, and he would easily get possession of the realm. She invited them, therefore, to repair secretly to England, to confer with her on the subject; charging them, however, to bring very few, if any, Norman attendants with them, as the English people were inclined to be very jealous of the influence of foreigners.

The brothers were very much elated at receiving these tidings; so much so that in their zeal they were disposed to push the enterprise much faster than their mother had intended Instead of going, themselves, quietly and secretly to confer with her in London, they organized an armed expedition of Norman soldiers The youngest, Alfred, with an enthusiasm characteristic of his years, took the lead in these measures. He undertook to conduct the expedition. The eldest consented to his making the attempt. He landed at Dover, and began his march through the southern part of the country. *Godwin* went forth to meet him. Whether he would join his standard or meet him as a foe, no one could tell. Emma considered that Godwin was on her side, though even she had not recommended an armed invasion of the country

It is very probable that Godwin himself was

Godwin's designs.   His address to the Saxon chiefs.

uncertain, at first, what course to pursue, and that he intended to have espoused Prince Alfred's cause if he had found that it presented any reasonable prospect of success. Or he may have felt bound to serve Harold faithfully, now that he had once given in his adhesion to him. Of course, he kept his thoughts and plans to himself, leaving the world to see only his deeds. But if he had ever entertained any design of espousing Alfred's cause, he abandoned it before the time arrived for action. As he advanced into the southern part of the island, he called together the leading Saxon chiefs to hold a council, and he made an address to them when they were convened, which had a powerful influence on their minds in preventing their deciding in favor of Alfred. However much they might desire a monarch of their own line, this, he said, was not the proper occasion for effecting their end. Alfred was, it was true, an Anglo-Saxon by descent, but he was a Norman by birth and education. All his friends and supporters were Normans. He had come now into the realm of England with a retinue of Norman followers, who would, if he were successful, monopolize the honors and offices which he would have to bestow. He advised the Anglo-

Saxon chieftains, therefore, to remain inactive, to take no part in the contest, but to wait for some other opportunity to re-establish the Saxon line of kings.

The Anglo-Saxon chieftains seem to have considered this good advice. At any rate, they made no movement to sustain young Alfred's cause. Alfred had advanced to the town of Guilford. Here he was surrounded by a force which Harold had sent against him. There was no hope or possibility of resistance. In fact, his enemies seem to have arrived at a time when he did not expect an attack, for they entered the gates by a sudden onset, when Alfred's followers were scattered about the town at the various houses to which they had been distributed. They made no attempt to defend themselves, but were taken prisoners one by one, wherever they were found. They were bound with cords, and carried away like ordinary criminals.

Of Alfred's ten principal Norman companions, nine were beheaded. For some reason or other the life of one was spared. Alfred himself was charged with having violated the peace of his country, and was condemned to lose his eyes. The torture of this operation, and the inflam-

Alfred's cruel fate.   Banishment of Emma.

mation which followed, destroyed the unhappy prince's life. Neither Emma nor Godwin did any thing to save him. It was wise policy, no doubt, in Emma to disavow all connection with her son's unfortunate attempt, now that it had failed; and ambitious queens have to follow the dictates of policy instead of obeying such impulses as maternal love. She was, however, secretly indignant at the cruel fate which her son had endured, and she considered Godwin as having betrayed him.

After this dreadful disappointment, Emma was not likely to make any farther attempts to place either of her sons upon the throne; but Harold seems to have distrusted her, for he banished her from the realm. She had still her Saxon son in Normandy, Alfred's brother Edward, and her Danish son in Denmark. She went to Flanders, and there sent to Hardicanute, urging him by the most earnest importunities to come to England and assert his claims to the crown. He was doubly bound to do it now, she said, as the blood of his murdered brother called for retribution, and he could have no honorable rest or peace until he had avenged it.

There was no occasion, however, for Hardicanute to attempt force for the recovery of his kingdom, for not many months after these transactions Harold died, and then the country seemed generally to acquiesce in Hardicanute's accession. The Anglo-Saxons, discouraged perhaps by the discomfiture of their cause in the person of Alfred, made no attempt to rise. Hardicanute came accordingly and assumed the throne. But, though he had not courage and energy enough to encounter his rival Harold during his lifetime, he made what amends he could by offering base indignities to his body after he was laid in the grave. His first public act after his accession was to have the body disinterred, and, after cutting off the head, he threw the mangled remains into the Thames. The Danish fishermen in the river found them, and buried them again in a private sepulcher in London, with such concealed marks of respect and honor as it was in their power to bestow.

Hardicanute also instituted legal proceedings to inquire into the death of Alfred. He charged the Saxons with having betrayed him, especially those who were rich enough to pay the fines by which, in those days, it was very customary for criminals to atone for their crimes. Godwin himself was brought before the tribunal, and

Godwin's trial. His costly presents to Hardicanute.

charged with being accessory to Alfred's death. Godwin positively asserted his innocence, and brought witnesses to prove that he was entirely free from all participation in the affair. He took also a much more effectual method to secure an acquittal, by making to King Hardicanute some most magnificent presents. One of these was a small ship, profusely enriched and ornamented with gold. It contained eighty soldiers, armed in the Danish style, with weapons of the most highly-finished and costly construction. They each carried a Danish axe on the left shoulder, and a javelin in the right hand, both richly gilt, and they had each of them a bracelet on his arm, containing six ounces of solid gold. Such at least is the story. The presents might be considered in the light either of a bribe to corrupt justice, or in that of a fine to satisfy it. In fact, the line, in those days, between bribes to purchase acquittal and fines atoning for the offense seems not to have been very accurately drawn.

Hardicanute, when fairly established on his throne, governed his realm like a tyrant. He oppressed the Saxons especially without any mercy. The effect of his cruelties, and those of the Danes who acted under him, was, however, not

Hardicanute's tyranny. His death. Final expulsion of the Danes

to humble and subdue the Saxon spirit, but to awaken and arouse it. Plots and conspiracies began to be formed against him, and against the whole Danish party. Godwin himself began to meditate some decisive measures, when, suddenly, Hardicanute died. Godwin immediately took the field at the head of all his forces, and organized a general movement throughout the kingdom for calling Edward, Alfred's brother, to the throne. This insurrection was triumphantly successful. The Danish forces that undertook to resist it were driven to the northward. The leaders were slain or put to flight. A remnant of them escaped to the sea-shore, where they embarked on board such vessels as they could find, and left England forever; and this was the final termination of the political authority of the Danes over the realm of England—the consummation and end of Alfred's military labors and schemes, coming surely at last, though deferred for two centuries after his decease.

What follows belongs rather to the history of William the Conqueror than to that of Alfred, for Godwin invited Edward, Emma's Norman son, to come and assume the crown; and his coming, together with that of the many

Edward invited to the throne.   His coronation

Norman attendants that accompanied or followed him, led, in the end, to the Norman invasion and conquest. Godwin might probably have made himself king if he had chosen to do so. His authority over the whole island was paramount and supreme. But, either from a natural sense of justice toward the rightful heir, or from a dread of the danger which always attends the usurping of the royal name by one who is not of royal descent, he made no attempt to take the crown. He convened a great assembly of all the estates of the realm, and there it was solemnly decided that Edward should be invited to come to England and ascend the throne. A national messenger was dispatched to Normandy to announce the invitation.

It was stipulated in this invitation that Edward should bring very few Normans with him. He came, accordingly, in the first instance, almost unattended. He was received with great joy, and crowned king with splendid ceremonies and great show, in the ancient cathedral at Winchester. He felt under great obligations to Godwin, to whose instrumentality he was wholly indebted for this sudden and most brilliant change in his fortunes; and partly impelled by this feeling of gratitude, and partly

| Edward marries Edith. | Godwin's difficulties |

allured by Edith's extraordinary charms, he proposed to make Edith his wife. Godwin made no objection. In fact, his enemies say that he made a positive stipulation for this match before allowing the measures for Edward's elevation to the throne to proceed too far. However this may be, Godwin found himself, after Edward's accession, raised to the highest pitch of honor and power. From being a young herdsman's son, driving the cows to pasture in a wood, he had become the prime minister, as it were, of the whole realm, his four sons being great commanding generals in the army, and his daughter the queen.

The current of life did not flow smoothly with him, after all. We can not here describe the various difficulties in which he became involved with the king on account of the Normans, who were continually coming over from the Continent to join Edward's court, and whose coming and growing influence strongly awakened the jealousy of the English people. Some narration of these events will more properly precede the history of William the Conqueror. We accordingly close this story of Godwin here by giving the circumstances of his death, as related by the historians of the time. The readers of

Story of Godwin's death.   His protestations of innocence

this narrative will, of course, exercise severally their own discretion in determining how far they will believe the story to be true.

The story is, that one day he was seated at Edward's table, at some sort of entertainment, when one of his attendants, who was bringing in a goblet of wine, tripped one of his feet, but contrived to save himself by dexterously bringing up the other in such a manner as to cause some amusement to the guests; Godwin said, referring to the man's feet, that *one brother saved the other.* " Yes," said the king, " brothers have need of brothers' aid. Would to God that mine were still alive." In saying this he directed a meaning glance toward Godwin, which seemed to insinuate, as, in fact, the king had sometimes done before, that Godwin had had some agency in young Alfred's death. Godwin was displeased. He reproached the king with the unreasonableness of his surmises, and solemnly declared that he was wholly innocent of all participation in that crime. He imprecated the curse of God upon his head if this declaration was not true, wishing that the next mouthful of bread that he should eat might choke him if he had contributed in any way, directly or indirectly, to Alfred's unhappy end. So saying, he put the bread into his mouth; and in the act of swallowing it he was seized with a paroxysm of coughing and suffocation. The attendants hastened to his relief, the guests rose in terror and confusion. Godwin was borne away by two of his sons, and laid on his bed in convulsions. He survived the immediate injury, but after lingering five days he died.

Edward continued to reign in prosperity long after this event, and he employed the sons of Godwin as long as he lived in the most honorable stations of public service. In fact, when he died, he named one of them as his successor to the throne.

THE END.

www.ingramcontent.com/pod-product-compliance
Lightning Source LLC
Chambersburg PA
CBHW032134230426
43672CB00011B/2336